ACCIDENTAL
ANCHORWOMAN

PRAISE FOR *ACCIDENTAL ANCHORWOMAN*

"The emotional rollercoaster of Melba's decades of living her life out loud, from nurse at Bellevue to broadcast news legend: the treat is the re-telling. PERHAPS an accidental anchorwoman, BUT an authentic journey from start to finish."

> —Carol Martin, WCBS-TV anchor; Detroit Free Press reporter; host of *Alive and Wellness,* on America's Talking cable network

"Melba Tolliver's memoir will amuse you, make you angry, and possibly shock you. It is a page-turner, filled with her reflections on pivotal moments in New York City and American race relations. Beyond her career, Ms. Tolliver reveals, in excruciating detail, deeply personal experiences that shaped her personality and guided her life decisions."

> —Randall Pinkston, former correspondent/anchor, Al Jazeera America; White House correspondent, CBS-TV News; general assignment reporter, CBS Washington Bureau

"Melba has used her storytelling gift to remind some of us and entice others to see how 'Chance, Choice, Change, and Connection' can impact your life. Her story is intertwined with humor, wisdom of the ancestors, Southern, Midwestern and Northern experiences that treat you to a view of American history you may have overlooked. Thank You Melba!"

> —Lisa Jackson, Education and Community Outreach Liaison, Savannah (GA) African Art Museum; former executive VP and general manager, 40 Acres and a Mule Musicworks; segment producer, *Wake Up with Whoopi* morning radio show, Premium Radio

"Weaving in experiences of the Great Migration, civil rights activism, and a changing media landscape, Tolliver shares how she found and then used her voice to critique and question, to advocate and educate, to appeal to and share stories of everyday people. An inside perspective on what it meant to break barriers and be the change."

> —Dr. Karen Dunak, Arthur G. and Eloise Barnes Cole Chair of American History at Muskingum University; author, *Our Jackie: Public Claims on a Private Life,* NYU Press, 2024

"Melba shares her story with singular wit and style, and the profound life lessons she learned. I'm not sure Melba 'tells all' but it doesn't get more personal than this!"

> —Marquita Pool-Eckert, former CBS News producer

"Melba Tolliver is a pioneer in American journalism. From her defiant afro to her sharp on-air skills, she has been a role model for untold numbers of eager young journalists. Her insightful and sometimes-raw memoir is chock full of what goes on in the rough-and-tumble world of local television news—particularly in New York City."

> —Hwesu Samuel Murray, Attorney, author of *African American Economic Development: A Plan for Black America*; former WABC-TV producer of *Like It Is*

"Melba is the best at anything she does and here we see an example in this memoir. Fun, funny, inspiring. A must-read."

> —Natalie Goldberg, author of *Writing on Empty* and *Writing Down the Bones*

ACCIDENTAL ANCHORWOMAN

A Memoir of Chance, Choice, Change, *and* Connection

MELBA TOLLIVER

Cataloging in Publication Data
Library of Congress Control Number: 2024912272

Tolliver, Melba
 Accidental anchorwoman: a memoir of chance, choice, change, and connection / Melba Tolliver

ISBN 979-8-9908448-0-3 (hbk.)
ISBN 979-8-9908448-2-7 (pbk.)
ISBN 979-8-9908448-1-0 (ebook)
ISBN 979-8-9908448-3-4 (digital retail)
ISBN 979-8-8751445-6-1 (digital library)

1.   Journalists—United States
2.   Race and Ethnic Relations
3.   Biography & Autobiography
4.   Tolliver, Melba

The events and conversations in this book have been set down to the best of the author's ability.

Audiobook narrated by Melba Tolliver. Recorded February through June 2024 at The Social Tour, 12 South Sitgreaves St., Easton, PA, 18042. Sound engineer, Justin Little. Audio editing, Andrew Laties.

Front jacket photo: *Portrait of Melba Tolliver,* Stephanie Brook. "An Angry Woman" photo, page 136, and text of "Appendix—An Angry Woman" reprinted from: Robert S. Bird, "Ten Negroes," *New York Herald Tribune,* 1963. Other personal photos courtesy of Melba Tolliver.
Cover design by Rebecca Migdal. Rebel Bookseller logo by Nolen Strals.

Printed and bound in the United States of America
First printing July 2024

Published by Rebel Bookseller, an imprint of: Book and Puppet Company, Easton, PA, USA, 18042

For
Susan Ola
my mother

Constance Louise
my sister

And Emory Leonard
my father

CONTENTS

Author's Note

Just days after I graduated high school my mother shipped me off to New York City to become a nurse. Being a good girl, I did what she wanted. I went to nursing school and became a registered nurse, a state board-licensed RN. After that I did what neither she nor I could have imagined: I became a TV news anchorwoman.

Early in my television news career on one of my mother's rare visits to New York City I arranged for her to spend some time with me at work. In addition to general assignment reporting for WABC-TV *Eyewitness News,* I also co-hosted the early am local news and interview program, *A.M. New York.* Rather than have my mother race around town with me and a camera crew on an afternoon assignment yet to be determined—thinking it might tire her out and make for a logistical headache—I opted to give her a ringside seat in the studio where she could watch Dan Daniels, my co-host, and me do the morning show, live. I made a place for her seated behind the two big studio cameras, out of their range but with an unobstructed view of our set, a make-believe living room complete with couch, coffee table, and a chair for a guest. Between talking over last minute changes in the program with the producer and getting a final pat of powder from the makeup lady, I shot a look in my mother's direction. I hoped she was impressed and enjoying her first time in a TV studio. I also prayed that I wouldn't make any gaffes. Or that she wouldn't pick up on them if I did.

Our first interview, the author of a children's book, could not have gone more smoothly. In the commercial break I snuck another peek at my mother, sitting so straight and turning to watch every time a cameraman or the stage manager made a move.

Next up, a female animal trainer accompanied by a baby lion cub who, despite his youth, kept tugging on his leash so hard that the trainer on the other end struggled to keep her attention on the interview. Near the end of the segment, the cub made one energetic, last lunge, toppling the trainer and her chair just as we went to commercial. Dan and I reacted the way any people with sense would: we ducked for cover. My mother, watching all this from the safe side of the cameras, let out a loud gasp before raising one hand to her mouth trying to stifle a hearty laugh.

She had just witnessed the unpredictability of live TV, and gained one more "Would you believe it?" story to share with the folks back home about her daughter's adventures in the big city.

After the show and our usual half hour post-mortem with the producer, I grabbed my things and headed off from the studio with my mother onto busy Columbus Avenue. She was still chuckling over the untamed cub catastrophe as we walked to a nearby coffee shop. While I held tight to her arm, pointing to the landmark Lincoln Center buildings a block away, she had a bright idea. I could almost see the light bulb go on over her head. "You should write a book, honey, about your wonderful life," she said, flashing a slightly crooked smile in her high-cheekboned face, the look in her eyes guaranteeing me at least one committed reader in the event I took her advice. As we slid into a booth, vinyl upholstered in her favorite color, red, she continued, "You could tell what it was like to be in the right place at the right time."

She was referring, of course, to the day in March 1967 when the ABC News brass, caught off-guard and flat-footed by a strike, drafted me, a network news secretary to fill in for a network news anchor. In a single afternoon I went from Melba typing memos to Melba reading the news on national television. Now, here was my mother—my most loving and influential role model for how to be an independent woman—challenging me to share that unplanned, unexpected, out-of-the-blue experience.

After more stops and starts than I care to count, I am once again, like my seventeen-year-old self, doing my mother's bidding. What I write could be read as simply the story of a "wonderful life" that she believed was mine. But I hope it will be more. As I share my experiences from the perspective of my ninth decade on this planet, I hope to pay tribute to the amazing grace and wisdom of ordinary, everyday people like the ones who raised me. I also hope it will illuminate my belief that each of our lives is full of wonder. All that's asked of us is that we pay attention, and that we stay awake to the constant interplay of chance, choice, change, and connection.

MELBA TOLLIVER

1—Booker T and Me

"Do you know where that name comes from?"

1957

"Tolliver?" asks the young white doctor. He is squinting in the direction of my chest and the name tag pinned to my student nurse's uniform, a starched white bib and apron layered over a blue-and-white-striped mid-calf dress paired with black shoes and stockings. My uniform is a modest update of the original Bellevue student outfit going back to the eighteen-hundreds. The doctor looks away from me momentarily, returning his attention to the patient's chart in his hand.

"Tolliver!" he says again, this time with authority, turning my last name into a statement of fact. He flips the chart closed, slips it into the holder hanging at the foot of the metal bed, and looks me full in the eye. "Do you know where that name comes from?" he asks.

"No, not really," I say.

I am unprepared for the doctor's question, just as I was unprepared for Bellevue Hospital when I'd arrived here. The place was like something out of a horror movie, ancient, ghostly, and sprawling over four New York City blocks. But that fact had cut no ice with my mother once she set her mind on making me a nurse. At seventeen, I had been hustled off to the nation's oldest and possibly scariest hospital whose very name—Bellevue—was shorthand for psycho. Though, in fact, its psychiatric unit on 30th Street was only one of the hospital's many departments.

"Most people with the name Tolliver come from the Carolinas or Virginia. And some spell your name with one 'L'," the intern continues as I follow him to the next patient who has an IV drip running into a vein in his arm. The patient is awake and looks worried.

"Tolliver was originally Taliaferro," the doctor says, rolling each syllable slowly off his tongue with military precision. "It means iron monger or iron worker in Italian. Taliaferro is what the 'T' in Booker T. Washington's name stands for," the doctor says, citing one of the most famous Black men in the history of America.

A Black man born into slavery, Washington gained his own freedom, and later earned national prominence in the nineteenth century as he traveled the United States, preaching a message of vocational training and entrepreneurship, especially for Southern Blacks experiencing their first taste of freedom after the Civil War.

Booker T. Washington predated my mother's generation. He died in 1915, a year after she was born, but no doubt she knew of his reputation as an educator, orator, and persuasive politician. Along with three younger siblings, my mother went to high school in Anniston, Alabama. Though born, raised, and living in segregated Cave Spring, Georgia, they were enrolled at Barber Memorial Seminary, a boarding school for Black children, thanks to the largesse of their elder sister, a nurse working in New York and sending part of her paychecks back home. At Barber the Turner children were likely to have been made aware of Washington and one of his severest critics, W.E.B. Dubois, as well as other influential Black Americans.

One thing for sure, my mother and Booker T. Washington shared a belief in practical education. And whenever I ran through the reasons why I didn't want to leave home in 1956, much less become a nurse, my mother rebutted my reasons with her standard closing argument: "You'll always have a job, honey. There will always be sick people. Just wait and see. You'll thank me one of these days."

2—Help Wanted Female

"Don't forget to smile."

"Melba!" That's Donald L. Coe, operations manager for ABC News, calling my name. Before I can get my coat off, he waves me into his corner office, a scowl replacing his usually sunny smile.

"These special credentials are for people allowed into the building during the strike," he says, handing me a bunch of plastic identification badges. "I want you to distribute them. Make sure they get to the right people."

It's a crisp March morning and a strike is the last thing I'm expecting to mess with me and my day. The American Federation of Television and Radio Artists (AFTRA) had threatened for months to pull the plug on contract talks with the three broadcast networks, but nobody on either side thought it would happen. Until it did. Now, in cities around the country, union members and their supporters have walked off the job at ABC, CBS, and NBC. The strike is the first in the union's thirty-year history.

I don't belong to AFTRA. I am not a radio or television *artist* by any stretch of the imagination. I am a secretary: a secretary of limited experience, at that, having only recently traded my operating room nurse's green scrubs for the buttoned-up uniform of the business world.

Don Coe is my boss, a white man in his early fifties. He personifies squeaky clean. His bald head and rosy cheeks have the fresh-scrubbed look of someone who just stepped out of a vigorous shower. He smells like a bar of Dial soap.

Six months earlier, when Coe interviewed me for the job as his secretary, he immediately put me at ease; he was friendly and showed a keen sense of humor. At the time I had held only one other secretarial job, a brief stint at Artra. A small company located in the boondocks of New Jersey, Artra made a laxative for women and a line of cosmetics for dark-skinned people. They also sponsored a televised Sunday morning gospel show.

Because I clung to the habit of staying in bed till the last minute, getting to work challenged me to a daily race at the peak of New York City's morning rush hour. On the first leg I half-walked, half-ran nine blocks from my apartment on West 149th Street to the nearest subway station, raced down the stairs to take the downtown A train to Times Square, and made my way to the Port Authority Bus Terminal, one of the city's biggest and busiest commuter hubs. Then, like a salmon swimming upstream, I pushed through the crowds of commuters heading in the opposite direction, they were coming into Manhattan and me trying to get out. On the best days I made it with minutes to spare, pulse racing and short of breath, to the commuter bus line and the one bus going to my destination. That bus, when it left Port Authority and headed west, was practically empty. Forty-five minutes later, it dropped me off in an area carpeted with manicured lawns and devoid of sidewalks, where I stood out like an ink spot on a blank page. The few white locals whose paths I crossed either looked past me as if I were invisible or gave me a "What are you doing here?" look. By the time I reached my desk I was half-spent. After several months of this routine, on top of still hurting from the pain of a busted romance, I started feeling a lump in my throat that I couldn't swallow.

"It's your thyroid," the first doctor I saw told me. "You need to have it removed," he said, wasting no time to add me to his surgical schedule. My best friend, Martha Starks, worked for this doctor, and because I was on a short trip back to Akron, Ohio, my hometown, I chose to see him. Reluctant to part with that vital part of my anatomy, I said I'd get back to him. Instead, I returned to New York and hurried to Bellevue Hospital where I knew from my student nurse days that doctors had seen just about everything from the rarest to the most mundane medical conditions on its wards and in its clinics.

"*Globus* is what you have," said the thyroid clinic specialist after reviewing my symptoms and examining my neck and throat—and hearing my commuting and heartbreak woes. Armed with what I took as good news, that my swallowing problem, *globus hystericus,* was caused by stress, and that I could keep my thyroid, I vowed to double my efforts to get over my infatuation with a married man who I had fantasized as Mr. Right. His wife had answered my last phone call to him. When he got on the line, he told me, "We're back together, so please don't ever call me again." The *globus* diagnosis also gave me reason to give two weeks' notice to Artra, ending both my awful early morning commute and, temporarily, my secretarial career.

No one could have predicted that I would ever work as a secretary again, or be working for Coe in 1967, least of all me. True, I knew how to type, but that was my singular secretarial skill, learned in high school where I chose not to learn shorthand. Later though, once I moved to New York and became a regular passenger and observer on its subways, I found I could easily decipher a popular advertisement posted just about eye level in nearly every subway car. "If u cn rd this," the ad promised, "u cn ern gd mny." Further along, in plain English, the ad invited straphangers on the A and D trains to sign up for a six-week course. I never followed up on that invitation, figuring "I cld lrn ths by mslf," if I ever needed to.

I did take action though on another ad. This one appeared one Sunday in the "Help Wanted Female" section of the *New York Times*. ABC News was hiring secretaries.

On the appointed day and hour, I joined a small group of white jobseekers at the ABC headquarters, a sleek high-rise at 1330 Avenue of the Americas, in midtown Manhattan. I took a seat in the personnel department reception area, filled out a few forms, handed over a resume, completed a short questionnaire, and waited. Before long, a middle-aged white woman in a tailored business suit ushered a dozen of us into a room equipped with earphones at each small station. Of all the would-be employees, I was the only one who mistook the setup for a hearing test. Everyone but me sat down to demonstrate their shorthand skills, or lack of them. Realizing I was out of my league, I asked to be excused and slinked back to the reception room, certain my name had just dropped to the bottom of the hiring list.

Still, I stayed, stubbornly turning a deaf ear to the nagging voice in my head: *Get real, Melba. You know you don't stand a chance of getting hired.*

The personnel people interviewed me a second time and reviewed my so-called work experience. They said they thought I would be a good fit for one of their executives and sent me across town to Coe's office at ABC News headquarters. The dull grey building at the corner of West 66th Street and Central Park West stood in stark contrast to THE Dakota, THE San Remo, THE Eldorado, and other storied apartment buildings that face the great park and where white doormen in military-inspired garb and white gloves act as imperial gatekeepers.

Taking dictation, it turned out, was nowhere on the list of Coe's requirements for his girl-Friday kind of secretary (and I never told him about the earphone fiasco). Coe explained that he drafted his correspondence on a black, antique-looking Remington manual typewriter that sat in the middle of his very neat desk. He drafted his letters and memos on the Remington and turned them over to his secretary who typed the finished versions.

Coe and I talked for nearly an hour. He listened carefully as I told him how I had moved to New York at age seventeen right out of high school to study nursing at Bellevue Hospital, that I had passed the state boards after graduation and had become a licensed RN. Coe nodded in all the right places when I explained that after a couple of years of passing scalpels and sponges, as a masked, gowned and rubber-gloved OR nurse, I felt I wasn't cut out to be a modern-day Florence Nightingale. "I want to do something else with my life," I said, without defining "something else."

I didn't tell Coe, but I thought working at ABC News might shed some light on my career options beyond secretary. I thought my interest in people and world events might lead to work as a researcher, and if he hired me as his secretary, I would work for him only long enough to find out.

I also didn't mention being written up in the *New York Herald Tribune* three years earlier. In April 1963, the *Tribune* had run a series titled, "Ten Negroes," promising "a powerful and provocative look at today's Negroes." I had looked forward to reading it. But after the first three articles—which I read on my daily commute to New Jersey—I found the series a big disappointment and said so in a scathing letter to Robert S. Bird, the newspaper's national correspondent and author of the series.

Soon after he received my letter, Bird called me and politely asked to interview me over the phone. He also asked if he could send a photographer to my home to take my picture. I said OK to both requests. A few days later, Bird wrote a conclusion to his series, and smack dab in the middle of his wrap-up was my letter and a picture of me looking very serious below a caption in bold letters that read, "An Angry Woman."

Bird wrote that his series had produced an avalanche of mail, much of it praise from readers, Black and white. About the negative mail, Bird wrote, "One of the bitterest, angriest and most contemptuous letters—and one of the most literate—came from a woman."

Now, three years later, ABC personnel had sent that "Angry Woman" letter-writer over to Coe's office where she and the former newsman turned news executive were having a pleasant conversation with no indication that he had ever seen the "Ten Negroes" series or if he had, that he made no connection between me and the letter-writer's caustic comments.

During the interview, Coe told me he lived in Greenwich Village with his wife, Hester. I told him I was married to Charles Attale, a New York City fireman, and that we lived in

Harlem. Coe said he and his wife's favorite vacation spot was the Caribbean Island of Jamaica. And I shared with him the fact that my husband's family had immigrated to the United States from Trinidad, also in the Caribbean. Coe and I went back and forth like that, talking and listening, making connections, and finding common ground. At one point, I told Coe that I had studied acting at the American Academy of Dramatic Art and the HB Studio in Greenwich Village, until I realized I was wasting time and money. It was obvious to me that I was too self-conscious and untalented to convince an audience, let alone myself, that I was a believable character. But given a chance to just be myself, I had managed to land a few non-speaking parts as an extra in some movies and TV commercials.

I liked Coe and I could tell he liked me, too. That's why as the interview was about to end, I felt an urgent need to confide in him something I had been holding back.

"I'm in the running to become 'Miss New York Is a Summer Festival,'" I told him. "And I think I have a good chance of winning," I continued, hoping he wouldn't change his mind about hiring me. "If I win, I would have to quit working for you because I would be off traveling around the country representing New York City and helping the Tourist and Visitors Bureau drum up business for the city."

Coe listened, nodding his head.

"I wouldn't worry about that," he reassured me. "You can cross that bridge when you come to it."

Maybe Coe thought my chances of winning the contest were slim. Or maybe in that moment he became a shirt and tie-wearing Zen master teaching me to deal with the present just as it is. Anyhow, Coe was right that I shouldn't worry. As it turned out, one of the other contest finalists—all of them white and five of them also nurses—got to represent New York City, and I got the chance to work for Coe.

Now, six months later, on this March day, striking news people are outside ABC headquarters, noisily discouraging others from crossing their picket line. Since mid-morning, Coe and half a dozen other executives have been meeting with Elmer Lower, president of ABC News, an imposing man with steel gray hair and the quick eyes of a no-nonsense veteran newsman. This all-white, all-male strike contingency committee, given the job of lining up substitute anchors, had named Sid Byrnes, a white man and network assignment editor, to fill the empty chair of Marlene Sanders, anchorwoman of *News with the Woman's Touch*. Something was definitely wrong with that picture. As Lower said to his men, "Sid Byrnes is not exactly what women want in the afternoon."

Neither did Purex, the show's sponsor and the makers of soap powder and other household products want Sid, or any other man, taking over for Marlene and *News with the Woman's Touch*. The program aired at two-fifty-five in the afternoon, following *The Dating Game*. It hung onto the large audience of housewives tuned into ABC at that hour, and despite the show's fluffy title and its time slot, it offered women five minutes of mostly *hard news*.

The demographics for *News with the Woman's Touch* had obviously escaped the attention of Lower's lieutenants, and now he had set about correcting their planning mistake. "Anyone know any women in the company with public speaking experience?" Lower asked. Silence.

The faces and names of every female secretary, typist, and switchboard operator in the company must have crossed the minds of the assembled executives before Don Coe spoke up.

"Well, my secretary has done some public speaking and been in a few films."

When Coe returns to his office from the strike crisis meeting, I am back at my desk, having carried out my assignment to distribute the special identification tags.

"Melba, come in here for a minute. I need to see you." Thinking he wants to talk about the ID tags, I pick up my list of names and step into Coe's office.

"Please close the door," he says and lowers his voice.

"Do you think you could sit in for Marlene today?" he asks, one hand straightening his tie, the other hand jingling some loose change in the pocket of his gray trousers. I take in Coe's words, but for a moment they refuse to register in my brain.

He asks again, "Think you could sit in for Marlene?" He goes on to say that the other executives drew a blank when Lower asked if anyone could suggest a woman in the company who might occupy Marlene's anchor chair for the day. And since Coe knew about my failed acting classes and my tiny list of TV commercial credits, he thought I could do the show and get through it without fainting.

"It will be just for today," Coe promises. He says that by the next day the strike contingency committee will find someone more qualified to be Marlene's replacement.

Could I be hearing right? Was Coe really asking me if I could go on national television as a news anchor? Was he talking to me who thought I wanted to be a researcher and only took the job as his secretary to get my foot in the door of a news organization?

Figuring that I would know in six months if I had what it took to do research, I had planned to nose around and ask questions. But the typing and filing, the answering and returning of phone calls, the completing of applications for correspondents' credentials, and handling other important-but-not-urgent work that found itself on Coe's desk, kept me too busy to play detective. I hadn't met a soul in research or talked to anyone about how one broke into that part of the news business.

Coe is waiting for my answer.

"Sure, I'd be happy to do it," I say, ignoring all reason as thoughts chase each other around in my head, all of them telling me to turn down his offer. The only thing I know for sure is it's March, my self-imposed six-month deadline is near, and I have made no progress in researching research as a possible career. So why not be an anchorwoman for a day? What do I have to lose?

"Sure," I say, tightening my grip on the identification tags list that I have forgotten and still hold in my hand. "I'll do it."

In the months that I have worked for Coe, I have never set foot in the news studio, or spent any time in the *Woman's Touch* office; never met the show's anchor, writer, or producer. I have not seen a news script or a TelePrompTer.

You must be crazy, the voice in my head announces, again. *You're agreeing to make a fool of yourself on national television,* the voice continues, just in case I missed its first message. The thoughts keep popping up like balloons in a carnival game of chance, and I keep trying to knock them down.

Maybe because things happened so fast. Maybe because I was being asked to step in for only one day. Maybe because it meant an exciting break from my humdrum secretarial work. Somehow, some part of me deep down inside, manages to overpower my negative thoughts.

Coe, knowing that I will need help if I accept his offer, has recruited Sonny Diskin, the director of Marlene's show, to give me a few pointers. As I battle my thoughts, Diskin ducks into Coe's office like a blue-eyed Irish genie, closes the door and checks to be sure it is shut.

Diskin takes a chair near Coe's desk and rattles off a few brief instructions.

"Listen, Melba, just read the script and smile a lot. If anything goes wrong—say, a switch to Chicago or Washington fails or the film doesn't come up when it's supposed to—we'll go to black. The stage manager will hand you some copy. Read it and then go on to the next page of script. Got it?"

I know "go to black" means deliberately losing the television picture. But I have no clue about a "switch" (introducing a news story in New York and switching to another location—Washington or Chicago in this case— where the film would be rolled on cue).

Then Diskin repeats his last bit of advice: "Remember, no matter what happens, don't forget to smile."

His briefing finished, Diskin hurries from Coe's office, trying hard to look innocent of the crime he has just committed. It's a big risk. If word gets out that Diskin has helped me, a scab, the strikers will brand him a traitor.

Coe tells me to drop whatever I am doing and report downstairs to the *Woman's Touch* office to get ready for the program. It is now just after twelve noon. The program is to air in less than three hours.

Armed with Diskin's instructions and Coe's directive to "Break a leg," I open the door to his office and feel the eyes of everyone who works on our floor on me. Word has leaked out that I am filling in for Marlene. As I straighten the papers on my desk, turn off my electric typewriter and gather up my purse, Carol, another secretary, rushes over, wide-eyed in disbelief. She stage-whispers, "Melba, are you *really* going to do it?" She can barely contain her excitement and launches into a barrage of questions. "When did you find out? Why did they pick you? Do your husband and family know? How long do they want you to substitute for Marlene? Are you nervous? Are you scared?" she asks.

I rush to answer. "No, I haven't told anybody. It just happened. I just said I'd do it. They're trying to get somebody for the rest of the strike. It's just for today. I'm not scared," I assure her.

But I am lying. I *am* scared. And I want to get away from Carol before she finds me out. If she sees through my bravado, she doesn't show it. She wishes me, "Good luck."

When I walk into the *Woman's Touch* office, trying to appear as if this turn of events is no big deal, Fred Sheehan, the show's producer, is at his desk.

The sleeves of Fred's white shirt are rolled up to his elbows. His face looks pinched around his mouth and his eyes are distant behind horn-rimmed glasses. I introduce myself, and Fred gives me a quick look before turning back to a pile of papers on his desk. Under ordinary circumstances the entire staff of the low budget *Woman's Touch* program consists of anchor Marlene, news writer Shirley Wershba, and Fred.

Off in a corner of the room, a line of wire-copy machines rattles non-stop. Spilling from the machines and onto the floor are rolls of white paper inked with words imprinted by keys of type transmitting the latest news from around the country and the world, wherever wire-service reporters are at work for the Associated Press, United Press International, and Reuters.

I pull up a chair to Fred's desk. He hands me a copy of the rundown listing the stories in the show and their running times, never looking directly at me. Fred and I are partnered in something neither of us could imagine when we left our respective homes this morning. I am about to spend five minutes reading the news to a nationwide audience. Fred is producing a news program for someone who has yet to work even one day as a novice newscaster, much less as an anchorwoman. And if that weren't enough, the woman is Black.

Fred puts the final touches on the script and hands me my copy. I read it once, twice, three times, ask a few questions, make notes in the wide left-hand margin, and underline hard-to-pronounce words and names that might give me trouble on the air. The simple act of marking up the script is calming; it gives me something to do, somewhere to put my attention, a way to quiet my head chatter.

Time to head over to the studio. *Woman's Touch* broadcasts out of a cavernous space on the ground floor of the Hotel Des Artistes. A New York City landmark, the Des opened its doors in 1917, never as a hotel, but as an artists' co-op. Ten floors of studio spaces are home to a mix of artists, musicians, actors, writers, and businesspeople. Actress Fanny Brice and movie idol Rudolph Valentino, dancer Isadora Duncan and artist Norman Rockwell have been some of its famous tenants. John Lindsay, the one-time mayor of New York City, and a glamorous figure in his own right, had once called it home. But the ghosts and glory days of the Des are far from our minds as Fred and I walk quickly from the ABC building, across sixty-seventh street to the Gothic structure and pass beneath its single gargoyle-ornamented façade, each of us deep in our own separate silent thoughts.

In the makeup area in a corner of the studio, I take a seat before a large mirror surrounded by naked light bulbs. I alternate between looking in the mirror, watching the makeup woman work, and re-reading my script. She powders down my face and brushes rouge on my cheekbones. She finishes and I take a tube of dark pink lipstick from my purse and do my lips. My hand shakes. I try to smile. My face feels frozen. I try again. Still stiff.

The studio is in semi-darkness, and it is cold. The set for *Woman's Touch*, off to the side of the studio, looks nothing like it appears on television. In real life it is small, and so flimsy that a brisk breeze could blow the thing down. The stage manager directs me to a chair behind the anchor desk and hangs a lavalier microphone on a cord around my neck. I take my seat under the lights hanging from the studio ceiling and feel warmed by their heat. Out front on either side of the stage manager, two cameras hold me in their blank stares.

I know none of the men behind the cameras. Not that it matters; they are not the regular cameramen. The regulars have walked off the set, in sympathy with the AFTRA strikers. If these management executive replacements had ever operated a camera before today, or handled audio, they haven't done so in a very long time.

"Can you read this?" asks a disembodied male voice from a far corner of the studio. The TelePrompTer operator wants us to do a trial read. He rolls the prompter, adjusting to my reading speed. I read the first page of the script. "Okay, okay," the voice shouts.

Another voice fills the studio. "Hi, Melba." I recognize Sonny Diskin speaking from the control room.

"This is Sonny. A couple of minutes and we'll be ready to go. Are you comfortable?"

"Hello, Sonny. Yes, I'm fine. I'm ready." I smile at one of the cameras. This is more like it. My face is slowly beginning to behave normally. I shuffle my script, make the pages into a neat stack in front of me, tighten my grip on a ballpoint pen in my right hand, and wait for more instructions from the control room. I close my eyes.

"Now's no time to go to sleep," Kenny the stage manager teases, smoothing his thick auburn moustache and leaning over the desk, his hand over the mouthpiece of his headset. Keeping his voice to a whisper, he repeats the instructions Sonny had given me earlier in Coe's office. "If we run into trouble with the switches, Sonny will go to black, and I'll be right here with the copy for you to read."

"OK. Thank you. Thanks a lot, Kenny."

"You'll do fine. Don't worry. And don't forget to smile," Kenny reminds me once more.

"Alright everybody." Now it is Sonny speaking again. "Here we go." Sonny sounds firm and reassuring.

The theme music comes up and my eyes follow Kenny's hand to camera one. I can see the first page of the script in the TelePrompTer just above the camera. Kenny begins to count down. "Nine, eight, seven," indicating the count with his fingers. "One." The camera tally light turns red. Kenny points a finger at me and spits out the last number with the force of a gun going off at the start of a one-hundred-meter race. I take a big breath. I feel my heart racing.

"Good afternoon. I'm Melba Tolliver sitting in for Marlene Sanders." I smile.

If I could have looked through the camera and into President Lower's office where he was watching the program, I'm certain I would have seen a shocked look on his face when he saw me, a Black woman, sitting behind the anchor desk.

Technically, the show is a disaster. We go two for two in the switch department: both switches fail. I introduce a report from Chicago. We go to black. Kenny hands me the prepared copy and I read it in a voice of sincere regret. "I'm sorry, but we seem to be having technical difficulty," I say, looking down at the copy and then up at the camera. I continue reading the next two pages of the script. I read the introduction to a report from Washington. We go to black again. Again, I apologize for the screw-up. The program ends and we redo it a second time for the West Coast.

It is finally over; the cameras are turned off, the lights dimmed. I stand up, a bit wobbly in the knees, exhilarated, breathless, pumped up, and drained all at once. I am happy I made it through, relieved the show is over, yet eager to try it again. I feel like my nine-year-old self back in Akron, Ohio, at the Summit Beach amusement park when I stepped down from my first roller coaster ride.

I haven't screwed up. I haven't made a fool of myself. I haven't embarrassed my mother and the rest of the family. People I don't know, but who might have been sitting on the edge of their sofa and chairs watching me, hoping for their sake and mine that I wouldn't stumble over a word or do something to make them cringe and turn away from their TVs, can let go of their collectively-held breath. I haven't let Don Coe or Elmer Lower down.

Why Coe had not brought up my race when he suggested me as Marlene's replacement was something he and I never discussed, but I wish we had. It seemed unimportant at the time. Only years later did I understand how much our choices and the chances we took mattered on that afternoon, when Lower and hundreds of thousands of viewers all over America tuned in to *News with the Woman's Touch* and witnessed something they'd never seen before: a Black person sitting at a network anchor desk, reading the news on national television. Lower hadn't known that I was Black when Coe raised my name at the meeting.

"I did not know whether you were Black, white or what. When I saw you, I thought we might have some problems with the Southern stations," Lower told me when I questioned him after he had retired, and I was writing this memoir. "In fact, we got some nice mail from the South," he said.

I return to the fourth floor and to a small crowd of secretaries and junior executives standing around my desk, smiling and offering congratulations. The phone on my desk is ringing, and I pick it up to hear a reporter on the other end calling from my hometown newspaper, the *Akron Beacon Journal*. The newspaper has already called my mother, something I had forgotten to do in the pre-show excitement. The *Beacon* reporter wants to know how I feel after my news debut on national television. The phone keeps ringing. It rings all afternoon. The Associated Press calls. The *World Journal Tribune* calls. They all want to hear from the secretary who was at her typewriter one minute and reading the news to the nation the next. They make it a Cinderella story. I have become a mini celebrity in one afternoon. The *World Journal* columnist, writing about the strike and the non-pros shoved into the limelight, describes Arnold Zenker, the CBS manager who takes Walter Cronkite's place, Darryl Griffin, an ABC news producer who is rushed in to replace Peter Jennings, and me. The columnist writes of me, "...a 26-year-old Negro who...didn't succumb to the wide-eyed stare of fright common to first timers." I like that part. But he screws up my name. He calls me Mabel.

In other parts of the country my TV debut has people talking, not in the newspapers, but over that oldest of media, the human grapevine. In a Cleveland beauty parlor, a client leans her head back into the shampoo bowl, gets set for her weekly wash, press, and curl, and asks her hairdresser, "Did you see that colored girl on TV doing the news this afternoon?"

"Yes," the shop owner, Rovena Coleman, replies with a mix of pleasure and pride. "That was Sue's girl—my niece, Melba."

When I get home that evening, still feeling the rush from all that's happened, my husband Charles has already changed from his fireman's uniform into street clothes. He is asking about dinner. He tells me everyone he knows is talking about me and my appearance on national TV.

"But what I want to know," he says, "What I don't understand, is why did you choose to use your maiden name on the air?"

3—Domestic Disorder

You aren't going any damn place.

"Melba, come here a minute," Charles calls out from our bedroom. I am in the living room, a short distance away from him, talking to my best friend, Martha Starks, and her husband Harvey. Martha and I have been best buddies since grade school. We had even planned to go through nursing school together. But the Universe, or whoever, had different plans. I got the nursing school experience while Martha stayed in Akron and got married. This was the couple's first visit to New York, and I had invited them to my home for lunch, expecting to catch up with the goings on in our lives and in our hometown where they still lived.

"Melba!" Charles calls again, this time in a louder voice.

"Excuse me, I'll be right back," I say as I get up and head to the bedroom. The door is half closed. Once I am inside the room, Charles reaches past me and pushes the door shut. His face is inches from mine. I feel his warm breath heavy on my face.

Wham! I don't see his hand before it swipes across my cheek, just missing my eye. The blow sends me staggering backward towards our bed. The muscles of Charles's face are tight. Sweat glistens on his forehead and the top of his shaved head.

"Who do you think you are inviting your friends here without asking me?" I swallow hard, grab a mouthful of air, and fight the urge to cry out. Or even speak.

Wham! This time I see his hand and I raise one of mine to shield my face. I am too slow. I feel a sharp pain as he strikes me with his open hand and his pinky ring scrapes across my cheek. I fall onto the bed on my back and look into his face. I still refuse to speak or cry. He bends over me and pushes his face closer to mine. Rage burns in his eyes and twists his lips.

"Answer me!" I pull away from him and rise from the bed. I think that if I keep silent Charles will stop hitting me. I think of Martha and Harvey only a few feet away. I hope they haven't heard the words, the punch, and the slap.

I straighten my skirt, pat my hair, and run a hand across my face. Charles lowers his hands and looks away. I turn from him and smooth the bed cover. He walks over to the closet, grabs a jacket, and walks out of the bedroom, through the living room, past Martha and Harvey, and out the door without a word.

Before returning to the living room, I duck into the bathroom, and under a stream of cold water, I wet a washcloth, wring it out and press it gently to my face. A large red welt has started to rise on my left cheek. Near my hairline a small cut has opened up.

Martha and Harvey sit quietly on the couch, looking as if the commotion in the bedroom hadn't reached their ears and that my roundtrip there had been only a minor interruption in our conversation. They look at my face and can't hide their embarrassment before they look away.

"Guess we'd better be on our way," Harvey says, breaking the silence and reaching for Martha's arm. She has been quietly studying the polished wood floor and now looks up and at her husband. She nods "Yes," and gathers up her purse.

I walk them to the door and step out into the hall. Martha lingers a moment as Harvey hurries down the stairs. Martha looks like she might burst into tears. Dare I let my own flow? Do what I hadn't been willing or able to do up to now? But Martha holds her crying in check and so do I. She gives me a big, hard hug. "I'll talk to you later," she says, more a question than a promise.

I stand in the hall, watching my friends disappear and wishing I were walking away with them, away from my home, away from my marriage, away to a place where I could scream and cry. A place where I would wake up from a bad dream.

Back inside the apartment I clear away the coffee cups and straighten the pillows on the living room chairs and sofa. In the kitchen I wrap a handful of ice cubes in a cloth towel, press it gently to my jaw, and feel the cold seep into my flesh and bones and mix with my hot tears. At last, with no one around to hear me, I let go of my humiliation, my shame, my anger, and let my sobs fill the room.

On Monday, I go to work as usual, acting as if nothing unusual was going on with me. The swelling on my face has mostly gone away; the cut near my hairline has turned into a black and blue bruise. "I was riding my bike in Central Park over this weekend and took a bad spill. It still hurts a little. But I'm OK. I just have to be more careful," was the explanation I had rehearsed in case anyone looked at me like they had a question. Only a couple of people do, and even if they suspect I am lying they pretend to buy my story. After all people fall off bikes all the time.

Charles never apologized. He never mentioned the incident—neither did I. The bruise healed, but our relationship couldn't. There was no doubt in my mind that our marriage was over. It couldn't be fixed. Small slights in the beginning of the marriage had escalated to angry accusations on both our parts and physical abuse on his. The day I continued walking down the aisle of St. Peter Claver Church I simply hadn't been ready to be a wife, not Charles's or anyone's. Now I faced the consequences of my choice to ignore the warning voice that spoke to me on my wedding day.

Our marriage had become a relationship of two nasty, opposing forces: Charles determined to control me and me showing him I would not be controlled. I resented his insistence that we spend holidays, most Sundays, and all of the family's birthdays and his niece and nephews' first communions at his mother's house in Brooklyn.

He had a car and took off whenever he pleased. I didn't drive and I had no car.

If I made plans to do anything without him, like go away with friends, he got angry and told me to stay home.

One time I made plans with Millie Bugg, a best friend and former Bellevue classmate who lived in Cleveland, to pick me up in Akron where I had been visiting family. And with her two young sons, we were to drive me back home to Harlem where I would re-pack my suitcase and then continue on to Oak Bluffs on Martha's Vineyard. I had made all the arrangements and looked forward to having a nice visit with Millie and her kids. But it was not to be. We got to my apartment where Charles was waiting. He was furious and stopped me from getting my things. Millie, meanwhile, was waiting in the living room, within earshot of Charles yelling, "You aren't going any damn place."

To keep the peace, I told Millie to go on to Oak Bluffs without me.

Things only got worse as Charles and I traded harassments and humiliation. One day as I stood at the kitchen sink, washing dishes, Charles walked up behind me, ran his hand up my dress, forced his fingers into my vagina, and accused me of cheating on him. It wasn't true. Another time, I went alone to a dance with a couple who were friends of both Charles and me. When the wife spotted Charles in the crowd, a few feet away from us, she tried to distract me with comments about some people sitting at a table in the opposite direction. But I had already seen what she wanted to turn my attention away from: Charles with another woman, and the two of them clearly looking like a couple.

I spent the evening pretending I didn't see what I was seeing. My friends dropped me off at home before Charles turned in for the night. And when he did, I confronted him in the bathroom and spit in his face. In another bathroom confrontation, he threw my contraceptive out the window before forcing himself on me while I lay face up on the bed and willed my body to go limp. He found his release on an unresponsive, silent, soulless corpse.

When we weren't finding new ways to insult and intimidate each other, we were mostly silent and sullen and taking great pains to stay out of each other's way. So, I felt relieved when at one point he enrolled in evening classes at the local college. Between work and school, and a business he had gotten involved in at a bar in Brooklyn selling Caribbean-style chicken wings on Friday and Saturday nights, he spent less and less time at home.

31

I reached a point where I began spying on Charles. Flipping through one of his textbooks I found an exchange of notes between him and a woman, along with a phone number. The next day I stayed after work and called the number from my boss's office.

When a woman answered, I told her I was Charles's wife, and that I would be divorcing him. A few days later he said to me, "So you're getting a divorce, huh?" This was his way of letting me know that he knew I knew he was seeing the woman.

We even took turns locking each other out of our apartment. The tactic generated business for the neighborhood locksmith but did nothing to make us quit hurting ourselves while trying desperately to hurt each other.

Throughout a year when my secretarial job became a news internship and then a trial position reporting for WABC-TV Channel 7, this was my domestic life. Day to day when Charles was around, I didn't know what to expect. I felt trapped in a minefield. Any step might be the wrong one and could blow up everything. I was happy to have him gone, and at times I wished he would just disappear, maybe have something happen at work, like die in a fire. No chance of that though since instead of fighting blazes he had become a buildings inspector for the fire department. That meant instead of pulling long shifts with overnights spent in the firehouse, he kept regular eight-hour days and came home at night.

I dreaded going home. And my work suffered. I was jumpy and nervous. I had trouble concentrating. I forgot stuff I should have remembered. It didn't take long for my boss to notice. I hurried to reassure him that I was fine when he asked if I was OK.

Things got so bad I even moved out briefly and stayed with a girlfriend who lived on Manhattan's West Side, two blocks away from ABC. That lasted until Charles called me at work one day and asked me to have dinner with him. I agreed and he spent the whole time apologizing for the beatings, the bitter arguments, the ugly accusations, and said he thought we could work things out. He said we should give the marriage another chance. And, reluctantly, I said I would give it a try.

Things didn't work out. Being away from Charles, even briefly, made me realize a divorce was the only solution for me. First, though, I went to his mother's in Brooklyn. Sitting at the kitchen table with her and two of Charles's older sisters, I told them what they might have already suspected, that Charles and I were constantly fighting (I spared them the details of his physical abuse), and I said that I just couldn't take it anymore. I said I wanted them to hear my side of the story from me. They listened but offered no advice or encouragement. When I got up to go, his mother let me out the front door without a word and I didn't look back. It was as if a fifty-pound weight had been lifted from my shoulders as I walked the few blocks to the subway and headed home.

Fred Samuel, the lawyer I went to for help with my divorce, had his office in Harlem on Striver's Row, the block of 138th Street between 7th and 8th Avenues. A dark-skinned jaunty little man, he explained New York divorce law, which didn't make things easy. I gave him a deposit and walked home. Again, I felt I was making the right choice. I was not yet ready to announce my intentions to the world. And certainly not to Charles, who would find out soon enough.

Seeing the lawyer renewed my sense of control over my situation. I concentrated better at work and felt less fear at home. I began thinking that breaking up with Charles would be easier than I had imagined. Once lulled into this complacency, I put off a follow-up meeting with my lawyer and gave most of my attention to work. When the Channel 7 news director offered me a fulltime job as vacation-relief reporter for his ABC local news station, I grabbed it before he could change his mind. My network internship was over. It took a while to believe that phase of my life was coming to a happy ending.

Now that I had a real job earning more money, I turned my attention to moving out of the Dunbar, and away from Charles. I thought I had found the ideal place in the Riverbend, a new apartment complex on 5th Avenue and 138th Street, still in Harlem. I qualified for the moderate-income co-op and took out a bank loan to finance the down payment. I moved from the Dunbar to the Riverbend in one afternoon, taking only my clothes, leaving the wedding china and silverware, the furniture, the books and everything else behind. I furnished the new one-bedroom space with a bed, a couple of lamps and a small color TV that rested on the box that it came in. The apartment was on the thirteenth floor, but I decided to make that my lucky number.

When Charles didn't try to contact me, and I didn't run into him anywhere, I thought he had accepted our split. I mostly put him and my divorce on the backburner.

I started getting comfortable in my new apartment. I adjusted to the changes at work. Ed Silverman, the man who hired me for vacation relief, was fired and replaced by Al

Primo who, based on rumor, was poised to remake Channel 7 and get rid of a bunch of people. Now was no time to worry about my domestic life, or so I thought. What I imagined as bringing order to my domestic disorder turned out to be the relative calm before the storm.

My friend Millie had given my phone number to a man she knew from New Jersey who wanted to meet me. I don't remember if she asked my permission to do that, but the man called and asked me out. I accepted. He asked again, and again I said "yes." At the time, I had been assigned to the late afternoon reporting slot, covering stories for the 11pm *Eyewitness News* program. One night, my new friend arranged to pick me up after I finished work. He was waiting in his car when I came out of the building. Suddenly, a second car pulled up, screeched to a halt, and blocked my new friend's car. I saw right away that it was Charles, stalking me. Before he could approach the other man, I stepped in and I told the other man to leave, that I would handle things. He hesitated, and perhaps hearing something in my voice, or seeing a look on my face, got in his car and drove away when Charles unblocked him. I was too angry and embarrassed to be afraid. I allowed Charles to drive me to my apartment but warned him that if he didn't stop stalking me, I would go to the police.

Time passed. My warning to Charles had apparently worked. He didn't show up again at my workplace, and I resumed seeing my friend. After a few more dates, I suggested that we go to Boston for the weekend. We spent a relaxing couple of days together and drove back home late Sunday. My friend decided to spend the night at my apartment, and we went to bed. We hadn't been in bed very long when suddenly the bedroom light came on, and there was Charles. I thought I must be dreaming. But no, this was real. Charles ordered me out of bed. That's when I realized he was not alone. Another man who I recognized as the boyfriend of one of Charles' sisters stood on the opposite side of the bed. He was holding a gun. He didn't say a word, just pointed the gun at my friend who had sat up in bed.

"Get into the bathroom," Charles said, waving his hand in the direction of the bathroom next to the bedroom. I did as he said. I was naked but didn't stop to cover myself; I just moved as fast as I could. Charles followed me. His accomplice remained in the bedroom, holding my friend at bay with the gun.

My bathroom was small. No place to hide. Nothing to cover myself. Charles began beating me, calling me names—keeping his voice low, like he didn't want people in the next apartment to hear him through the walls.

"Stop. Stop. Please. Stop," I cried over and over.

He didn't stop. And my pleading seemed to anger him even more. I tried to ward off his blows. I covered my face with both hands, but Charles pushed them away and struck me several times across my nose, my lips, and my forehead. His breathing was rapid and heavy. When he finally quit hitting me, he called me a few more vile names and left the bathroom. I fell to the floor, crying.

"Oh, God. Oh, God. Oh, God," I sobbed between gasping for each breath.

I never heard Charles and his accomplice leave. I only knew they were gone when my friend came into the bathroom.

"Are you OK?" He wrapped a bed sheet around me and led me back to the bedroom.

"I can't stay here. I've got to get out of here," I cried when I could finally speak. My whole body quivered, tears ran down my face and I struggled to catch my breath.

I managed to get dressed with my friend's help and he drove me to a motel, checked me in and stayed with me until I calmed down. Neither of us said much. We were both in shock. Without looking in a mirror, I knew my face was pretty messed up, but I felt lucky to be alive. Lucky that Charles's accomplice hadn't used his gun on my friend or me. My friend said he was going home and that he would call me in the morning and come back later in the day, Monday.

I was due at work that afternoon. No way was I leaving the motel and going back to my apartment, or to work. Instead, I called the office and asked to speak to the news director.

"Hello, Al. This is Melba. I won't be in today. I was in a car accident. I hit my head. My face is bruised. The doctor says I should take it easy a couple of days. I feel awful. But I should be back to work in a few days. OK?" The words came out in a stream before I took a breath.

"OK, Melba," Primo said slowly. "OK, I'll let the desk know. Just one thing, I'm not going to be embarrassed, am I?" His question and measured tone let me know that he didn't believe me. "You take care, now, and let us know if you need anything."

"OK. Thanks, Al." I hung up the phone and burst into tears. I stayed curled up in my bed, crying for a long time.

My friend called a couple of times during the day and showed up that evening with medicine to treat my cuts. Mostly he just held me, patted me, and reassured me. "It's going to be OK. It's going to be OK." He asked what I wanted to do. Go home? File a police report?

I was confused. I definitely was not ready to go home. I was afraid to be alone. I definitely didn't want friends to know what had happened or to see me in bad shape. And I didn't want to bring the police in either. I just wanted to stay curled up, hoping to go to sleep.

Thursday, I returned to work. Makeup camouflaged some of the bruises on my face. And I stuck to my "car accident" story. Friday, bright and early I found out where to go to get a restraining order. Afraid someone would recognize me, I wore dark glasses, and stood in the back of the room. But seeing other women—some of them obviously battered—seated and waiting to be called on, I felt I just couldn't go through the humiliation of confessing to a stranger, in public that my husband had broken into my home and beat me up. *I just can't do it. I can't,* I told myself. And I didn't.

Instead, I got back in touch with the divorce lawyer and picked up where we had left off nearly a year before. I told him about the break-in and beating. He didn't seem surprised.

After a couple of delays, I finally had my day in court, the Supreme Court of the State of New York. Two months later, the judge, noting that I had "complied with the conciliation proceedings specified in the Domestic Relations Law," granted me a divorce "on the ground of the acts of cruelty and assault committed by the defendant upon plaintiff."

Charles, the "defendant," had failed to respond to the divorce summons served nearly six months earlier and didn't bother to show up in court to hear the decision.

November 1970 brought an official end to a marriage not made in heaven. It cost five-hundred-and-thirty-five dollars for the divorce lawyer. The emotional and physical toll on me was harder to calculate.

I would see Charles a couple of times over the years. The last time I heard anything about him he had died in a Texas hospital waiting for a heart transplant.

4—Who's News

Keep pedaling, honey, just keep pedaling.

As 1938 drew to a close, Susan Ola and Emory Leonard
Tolliver, both in their mid-twenties, were living in Rome,
Georgia, a small hill town in the Northeast corner of the
state. On the other side of the Atlantic Ocean, Hitler and the
Nazis had occupied Czechoslovakia. In the United States,
Joe Louis had triumphed over Germany's Max Schmeling
with a first-round knockout. Sister Rosetta Tharpe, singer
and guitarist, was recording "Rock Me," and appearing with
Cab Calloway at Harlem's Cotton Club. On the site of the
upcoming New York World's Fair, the Westinghouse
Company had buried a time capsule fifty feet underground,
the capsule to be opened five thousand years into the future.
And on Halloween eve a radio drama of H.G. Wells's *War of
the Worlds,* performed by Orson Welles and his Mercury
Theatre of the Air, had spooked countless Americans with
news of a Martian spaceship landing in New Jersey.

Six weeks after Welles's make-believe news hit the
national airwaves, the Tollivers made news of their own.
Theirs was strictly local. At McCall Hospital, just after dusk
on Thursday evening, December eighth, my mother ended
her long labor with a final contraction and pushed me out of
my comfortable first home and into the bright lights of the
delivery room. While not the stuff of headlines, word of the

Tollivers' firstborn, after two miscarriages, drew smiles and "Praise the Lords" from family and friends alike. One more colored citizen was added to the rolls of Floyd County, Georgia.

Two years later, my parents and I became part of a much larger news story. This one, a remarkable nation-changer, came to be known as the Great Migration. Writing about it decades later, in her masterwork, *The Warmth of Other Suns,* prize-winning journalist Isabel Wilkerson described the migration as perhaps the most underreported story of the twentieth century.

No newspapers or magazines wrote about my mother and me or took our picture when she bundled me up and moved from Rome, Georgia to Cleveland, Ohio. Only the family made a big deal of my father returning his bell hop's uniform to the Forrest Hotel and reuniting with his wife and child up North a few months later. We Tollivers were mere statistics, anonymous, daily drifts of Americans who formed a massive torrent of Black folks leaving their homes in Georgia and Florida, Alabama and Mississippi, Texas and the Carolinas, and nearly every other Southern state between 1916 and the 1970's.

The Black newspaper world, most notably the *Chicago Defender,* reported and even encouraged the migration. When politicians and manufacturers in the North were changing their attitudes about hiring Blacks, the *Defender* encouraged folks to go for it! In white mainstream publications, this historic migration—by any measure, the largest internal movement by a single group of Americans within US borders—hardly caused a ripple.

Susan Ola, 1950s

Emory Leonard "E.L." Tolliver, 1940s

Unlike a car pileup on a major highway or a tornado ripping cross country, news generated by the Great Migration unfolded quietly, in stages. It was news that gathered and collected itself in slow motion. The disassembled, unrelated kinds of news that only those most awake and aware would be able to piece together, to appreciate the depth and breadth of the story the news was telling. And then to foresee the impact and consequences of millions of Black Americans on the move. Black Americans taking chances, making choices and bringing about change. Change, that like the receding tide, leaves nothing untouched in its wake.

Seen through the rearview mirror of history, the migration was the news-making headline-deserving saga of entire generations uprooted at once, or families, sometimes one person at a time, leaving the only homes they had ever known. Everyday people were changing a nation while not calling attention to themselves. They were people who remained mostly invisible—and certainly nameless—to the powers-that-be. They were history makers, ignored by headline writers—over fifty years of their story (de facto, the history of America)—in the very country they were changing.

Folks like mine left home not because they got fed up with *one* thing. It was not *one* segregated water fountain or movie theatre or five-and-dime store. It was not *one* lynching of a Black man who looked "the wrong way" at a white woman. It was not *one* Black woman forced to step aside so a white man might pass or relinquish her seat on the bus for his comfort. Not *one* school with its used textbooks or no books at all for Black children. Not *one* time being reminded that Black people had no rights that a white person—man, woman, or child—was required to respect.

Not *one* thing, but the accumulation of things, the piling on of slights and laws. The combined crush of a Jim Crow caste system created to keep Black people at the bottom of a ladder that barred them from putting a foot on even the lowest rungs and dared them to complain out loud or show up at the county courthouse and try to vote for change. Not one thing, after three-hundred years of enslavement, was enough to abandon all you knew and risk further uncertainties. What drove them away was the weight of it all, the slow erosion of their human beingness like the constant drip-drop, drip-drop of water wearing away stone.

By their absence, the leave-takers changed the places they left behind. Those Southern enclaves could no longer be sustained on the backs of exploited labor. The Southern horn of plenty would not be as fruitful with workers gone. While in the new places they chose to call home, the migrants' presence reshaped the labor markets, the culture, the demographics, and more. Cities like Los Angeles and Oakland, New York City and Newark, Detroit and Chicago benefitted from anxious waves of laborers. And myriad cities and towns on the way to those destinations acquired new residents as well.

In old trunks, tied-up bags, string-wrapped boxes, and even newly acquired suitcases, the leave-takers carried the most valuable things they owned: remnants of their dignity and pride.

In their heads and hearts, they carried those things that cannot be catalogued: the dreams that drove them to the far side of the Mason-Dixon line, and a willingness to cross over by train, bus, car or anything smoking.

My parents chose to put down new roots in Cleveland, not because they knew a lot about Northeast Ohio, but because other relatives found the city first. Family sent word that encouraged Susan Ola and Emory Leonard to make the move and take a chance. And there was work. My father got a job as a chauffeur. My mother joined her older sister as "help" in the homes of well-to-do white families. It was a start.

While my parents worked, I spent my days and nights with my grandmother Cora. My mother's mother came up to Cleveland from Cave Spring, Georgia, at the insistence of her adult children after her husband, Dallas Coates Turner died. Dallas provided for his wife and eleven children for many years by working as a chef at the local school for the deaf. And at the local hotel, Dallas playing guitar with his brother-in-law Dooley on the fiddle provided entertainment for the town's white folks.

Grandmother Cora (Gran-mama is how the word came out of my mouth) was the only girl in her family. She earned a teaching certificate and taught the neighborhood Black children. Many of her youthful days were spent reading books, learning to sew neat stitches, embroidering initials and tiny flowers on napkins and handkerchiefs, and crocheting doilies for tabletops and chair backs. Grandmother Cora's own mother, known to the locals as "Miss Sue," was cut from a different cloth. Miss Sue packed a pistol and had a way with a phrase, especially for people she considered backstabbers or sneaky gossips. When one of those folks crossed her path and greeted her with a sweet, "How you doin', Miss Sue?" she gave them a knowing look and tart reply, "I do some. I leave some. I don't do half the niggers say I do."

Miss Sue was long gone by the time I came along, but she lived on in family legend and in my mother who inherited her name, along with some of Miss Sue's "don't mess with me" personality.

My Gran-mama Cora, still a beauty in her sunset years, had wavy white hair and skin as smooth as chocolate pudding. Whenever she held me close my nose filled with the sweet smell of lilac talcum powder rising from her bosom. She loved giving hugs and had a gift for magically treating childhood ills. Chronic earaches? She eased my suffering with drops of sweet oil. Sniffles and colds? She doctored those nasty germs with a ready supply of castor and cod-liver oils. And if a cough looked like it was getting the best of me, she knocked it out with a layer of Vicks salve. She gently rubbed it on my chest and then covered me with a flannel rag heated up in the oven. The combination warmed me inside and out and blissfully sent me drifting into dreamland.

Every morning, except for Sundays or important holidays, Gran-mama exchanged her long nightgown for a floral-printed cotton house dress. She tied a bibbed apron over it and slid her feet into the backless slippers she deemed house shoes. When other days called for her to dress up, she paired one of her fine tailored white blouses with a simple black or navy-blue suit, and pinned a small gold-plated watch, the size of a quarter, on the jacket just above her heart. Weekdays, well before I woke up, she could be found in the kitchen stationed at the gas stove, hand on one hip, making breakfast, usually grits, scrambled eggs, bacon, and toast. Later in the day, she would again be at the stove stirring a pot. Or she would be sitting at her beloved sewing machine, head bent, one foot working the metal treadle, both hands guiding a seam in a dress or pair of trousers. On laundry days she would be standing erect alongside the waist-high ironing board sprinkling water over my Uncle Albert's white dress shirts and placing them in a neat pile of other rough dry clothes.

Before putting the hot iron to work, she tested its readiness with a tongue-moistened forefinger. All the while she hummed. "The Old Rugged Cross" and "His Eye Is on the Sparrow" were two favorites. She and I also listened to the radio, a cathedral-shaped wood-encased technology that kept us in touch with the soap opera antics of *Fibber McGee and Molly, Just Plain Bill, Stella Dallas, Backstage Wife,* and *Lorenzo Jones.* These were characters my grandmother followed every day and whose life stories she knew almost as well as her own. She could report who did what, where, when, why, and with whom. I learned to follow these audio souls and their trials and tribulations, too. For news, she tuned into H.V. Kaltenborn, the ex-*Brooklyn Eagle* reporter. The year I was born he worked for CBS and reported on the crisis in a place overseas called Munich. According to the historical records, that event gave credibility to both Kaltenborn and radio news.

During the war years at my grandmother's, I showed a strong, unexplained fondness for the Glen Miller orchestra. I could be asleep, but if their music drifted from the radio speaker, I sprung up wide-eyed and awake, listening. Equally unexplained was my fear of the iceman. He seemed a huge dark presence, his black leather patch laid across one shoulder below a hulking block of ice grappled with a pair of fierce looking tongs. I screamed whenever he showed up, screamed as he shoved the ten-pound ice mass into the top compartment of our ice box, and I didn't stop screaming until the poor man left.

Back when adults believed children should be seen and not heard, I was an only child straddling two households. My Aunt Rovena, a newly licensed hairdresser, owned the two-family house and lived downstairs. Upstairs, Gran-mama tended to things while my uncle Albert attended a school that taught him to make false teeth and set up his own dental lab. Between the two households, I was privy to grown-up conversations. I heard adult thoughts and opinions on all sorts of subjects, especially The War. When my folks spoke new words, the words—if not their meanings—went straight into my vocabulary: rationing, air raids, silk stockings, soldiers, oleo, and Roosevelt. The way they put words together made me want to try. Even though I didn't always understand what was being said, I knew these were phrases and folks the grownups often feared. I heard them talk about Pearl Harbor and what happened there on December seventh, the day before my third birthday.

One night after my weekly bath, my grandmother toweled me off, lotioned me up, and left me to put on my gown. That task accomplished, I ran barefoot from the lighted bathroom into the darkened bedroom and jumped feet first into her big bed. A loud crash followed. "Gran-mama, Gran-mama, the Japs got us. The Japs got us," I screeched. The slats holding up the mattress on the bed frame had given way, dumping Gran-mama onto the floor, with me draped around her neck. My reporting proved mistaken, but my instinct for the tabloid headline was right on.

Before long, my parents' job prospects looked considerably brighter in Akron, thirty-two miles down the road. Reason enough to pack up everything and move again, this time with a second baby girl, my sister Constance Louise. From day one, people "ooohed" and "aaahed" over my little sister. "She looks just like E.L.," they usually said, keeping to the old Southern tradition of reducing a man's first and middle names to a set of initials. "Just look at that sweet girl. She sure got them E.L. eyes."

In those days, the factory towers for Quaker Oats helped define Akron's skyline. The smell of just-milled oatmeal flavored the air. But it was the half a dozen tire-manufacturing companies, the Goodyear blimp, and the main street paved with rubber that earned Akron its title, "Rubber Capital of the World." Neither of my parents ever worked for the tire giants, but almost everybody they knew did.

Akron proved a good place for us, at first. We lived in North Akron, on Lods Street, in a house of squat rooms and dim ceiling lights, up the hill, past Jack's Grocery. This store, whose modest assortment of penny candy drew even the smallest neighborhood children, was perched at the top of a very long flight of concrete steps.

After a year in the rubber city, my parents' marriage started to fray. Harsh words escalated to all-out combat. In their bedroom, late one night I stepped in between them, trying to push my father away. Instead, I caused his balled-up hand to miss its mark and swipe a cluster of perfume bottles, scattering them across the dresser before they fell and smashed to pieces on the bare wood floor. The mixed scents of smoky Tabu and flowery Chantilly hung in the air of their bedroom for days after they made up.

Another time, in yet another fight, my mother ran to a neighbor's for help, followed by my father who broke in the back door. My mother was ready when he reached her, and she floored him with the neighbor's end table. "It made me so mad," she said, remembering the incident years later. "Most of my paycheck that week went to buy them a new table."

In the only picture I have of my father with Connie and me, he is on furlough from the Army. A roving photographer snapped it as we strolled down Main Street one July afternoon. In that photograph, my father wears a khaki uniform and a garrison cap at a rakish angle over his close-cut hair. I am a head taller than Connie who comes up to my father's waist. She and I wear wild rose-patterned cotton dresses and worried looks. We clutch small bags of something, popcorn perhaps, or Planters Peanuts. Our three-braid hairstyles look freshly done. My father is movie-star handsome, a ringer for actor Billy Dee Williams, and the look in his eyes—eyes prone to roving—say, "I'm good-looking and I know it." And by all accounts, he bragged that my mother was a lucky woman to have him. When she finally got fed up with the insults, the fighting, his fondness for whiskey and other women (she once confronted him in flagrante in a hotel room and made him hand over his cash before he spent it on the other woman), she divorced him.

He moved back down South and re-married. That walk down Main Street would be the last time Connie and I would see our father alive.

He was murdered in 1949. I grew up never knowing which of two different stories about his death to believe. In one, he tried to break up a street fight and the killer slashed his throat. In the other, a jealous husband knifed my father in a case of mistaken identity. No matter which is true, on a hot and humid July afternoon, my father's life slipped away from him as he bled to death on a sidewalk in Dalton, Georgia. Nobody ever paid for the crime.

My father's sister, the one we called Nanny Retha, phoned and broke the news to my mother. She slowly returned the phone to its cradle, went upstairs to her bedroom, lay face down across the red satin bedspread, and cried, quietly, for a long time. I watched from the doorway, wishing I could ease her heartbreak.

Once my parents moved North, my mother never set foot in the South again. "I didn't leave anything down South," she used to say on the rare occasions someone suggested she at least visit, maybe take a sentimental journey back home. But she was satisfied to have just her memories of the best things about her Georgia growing-up. She shared those with her girls. "Momma, tell us about back in the good old days," was the only prompt she needed from Connie and me. She was quick to retell tales of life before telephones and TV. She got a kick out of describing how she and her siblings raided the neighbors' fruit trees. She showed us how they stuffed their mouths with Damson plums and tried to lick up the fruits' juices before they trickled between their fingers and ran down to their elbows. Or she would recall her mother's knack for making the most of whatever material things the Turner family had—the oranges and peppermint candies that got doled out at Christmas—the breakfast biscuits, one for each child, that no one ever relinquished even when they were sick. And the shirts, pants, and dresses that got handed down until the clothing was threadbare and only good for the family's rag bag. She painted word pictures that let us imagine her, and my aunts and uncles, as kids who could get a fire going in the big woodstove all by themselves. Anything else about the South, about living under American-style apartheid, was a closed chapter she never talked about. Her one concession was to allow Connie and me to visit Georgia a couple of times to spend time with our Southern kinfolk on my father's side and to experience for our young selves what it felt like to move to the back of the bus or train at the Mason-Dixon line, drink from the separate water fountains for colored and white people, and go to the movies at a segregated theatre where Blacks took the back stairs to the balcony.

In Dalton for my father's funeral, Connie and I stood out from our other Georgia relatives. We were E.L.'s kids from up North who talked funny and picked at our food. Connie and I traded looks of disbelief from behind steepled hands during Grandma Katherine's blessing of the breakfast table, loaded down with chicken and biscuits, eggs and sausage, fried fish and grits, and gravy. To a couple of kids used to a bowl of Rice Krispies or maybe cornflakes with milk and sliced banana as our first meal of the day, this enormous spread looked less like breakfast and more like supper!

My father's widow, the cross-eyed and childless Louise, nearly started a major incident after my father was lowered into the ground. She said to Connie, "I think I'm gonna keep you, you look so much like your daddy."

One phone call to my mother back in Akron set things right. "Don't you worry, baby," she assured Connie. "When Retha and Melba head back home you'll be right with them. You can be sure of that."

My sister's other concern—we both tried every way we knew how to avoid looking at our father laid out in his coffin in the living room of the house we stayed in—was her shoes. They were new, a pair of blue suede, and she stepped carefully, trying to keep them out of the red Georgia clay.

When Momma and Daddy separated, my mother became a single parent with few good choices. She made the hard one of living in a rented room and paying Nanny Retha to keep Connie and me during the week while she worked a full-time job, pressing clothes and altering pants and dresses in a dry-cleaning plant. Nanny Retha, lived in North Akron, in so-called "garden projects," an assortment of two-story buildings, minus the gardens but given the name just because, or just in case.

Retha, her sons, Gene, David and Donald, and Connie and me, made her small second-floor apartment pretty cramped. When my mother had a little extra money, she bought special food for Connie and me, a box of Wheaties or Kellogg's Corn Flakes, to take with us when she dropped us off on Sunday nights. We didn't always get to eat our treats, though, because our cousin Donald sometimes got to them first. Donald was the youngest of Retha's boys and the fattest. We could always tell when Donald was coming into the apartment. You could hear him huffing and puffing up the stairs. Except for school, Donald didn't go out much. He was too fat to play baseball or football with the other boys in the neighborhood. His brothers, both normal size and athletic, didn't encourage Donald to go outdoors with them, even though Retha was always scolding, "You boys, take your brother with you. That's no way to treat your brother." But Gene and David pretended not to hear her.

Donald had a mean streak. There were times when Connie and I were left alone with him, and he took his frustrations out on us. He would expose his privates, masturbate and threaten to get us in trouble if we told. We never did. One time he opened the kitchen window and said he was going to hang one of us out the window by our heels. He never followed through on that particular threat. Connie and I learned early on that it did no good to report Donald's antics to Retha. Whenever we tried, she always took his side or found some excuse for his behavior. "He didn't mean no harm. You know Donald's just teasin'.'"

Easy-going as she was with her sons, Retha was strict with Connie and me. Especially when it came to food, she exercised "Retha's rules," and enforced the worst one over breakfast. In winter the meal never varied: a bowl of oatmeal, a fried egg sunny side up, a piece of toast and a glass of milk. We ate at the kitchen table, listening to Donald slurp down his food and trying to ignore the way he ate his egg. With the pointed end of his toast, he would break the egg yolk, then sop up the runny, yellow liquid with the bread. The sight of the egg yolk running into his plate turned my stomach. And I hated the taste of oatmeal even when Retha called herself "making it better" by sprinkling a spoonful of sugar on top of it. I almost always left the egg and oatmeal. And they were always waiting for me when I came home from school at lunchtime. By then, the egg was stiff, a slick glaze covered the oatmeal, and both were ice cold. I was supposed to eat the hours-old remains of breakfast before I could have lunch. Sometimes I was lucky: Retha would be out shopping, the other kids would be playing or fighting with each other, and I could sneak into the bathroom and flush the eggs and oatmeal down the toilet.

A home of her own was the goal my mother set for herself early on. And every payday, after settling what she owed Retha for keeping Connie and me, and paying her own room rent and expenses, she put aside whatever money was left. When she had saved up most of a fifty-dollar down payment, she borrowed the rest of the money from her younger brother, Clyde, took out a five-thousand-dollar mortgage and bought a small piece of the American dream.

It was a neat three-story house. Maroon-speckled asphalt shingles covered the outside. A driveway between our house and the Burtons' next door belonged to us but went unused because we never owned a car. Had there been a sidewalk, it would have met our yard. Instead, cracked concrete pavement fronted three yellow brick steps that rose up to meet a wooden front porch that stretched across the width of the house. On one end sat a metal glider, its hard curves softened by colorful flower-print pillows that my mother either sewed herself or scooped up from the bargain bin at the local Goodwill. A small back porch overlooked a weed-filled backyard around which my mother put up a stockade fence, soon as she could afford it. Combative neighbors who overlooked our yard occasionally threw things into it, things like an odd saucepan or a doll's headless torso, when they were not otherwise engaged from Friday night to late Sunday in alcohol-fueled, intergenerational fighting that involved fists, broken liquor bottles, and loud, colorful cursing. I watched their fights feeling a mix of curiosity: which member of the feuding family would throw the next punch, or what type of flying missiles would come hurtling into our yard. "Melba! Get in this house," my mother would call when she saw me on our back porch watching people clobbering each other. "How many times do I have to tell you to stay inside, don't be outside watching when those people start acting up? You're so hard-headed."

Our new house also had an attic that we used to store family stuff like scrapbooks that held neatly mounted black-and-white photos of well-dressed children, coquettish women, and good-looking stylish men. There were all kinds of odds and ends up there too. One we never quite figured out was an old stereoscope that when you looked through it turned ordinary pictures into 3D. That was fun even if we didn't know how the darned thing worked. Sometimes we turned part of the attic into a peaceful neighborhood for a two-story metal dollhouse that Connie and I peopled with paper dolls, entertaining ourselves for hours. But the attic was off limits in summer when it got hot as a sweat lodge up there, or in winter when it felt the way we imagined the North Pole to be.

In our basement, we stored bikes, held an occasional birthday party and washed and ironed the laundry. Lined up next to the washtubs and washing machine my mother stationed her Singer sewing machine, the thing she spent hours with and loved as much as anything she owned. A ping-pong table which my mother claimed to have bought for Connie and me was usually covered with yards of fabric. Simplicity patterns and straight pins waited for her to pick up where she'd left off on her latest sewing project. She sometimes shooed us down to the basement to practice our lessons on the rented violins she hoped we would someday learn to play. "You guys sound like two cats screeching," she would complain if we started fiddling within earshot of the kitchen after a particularly hard day at the dry cleaners. "That noise is getting on my nerves."

Best of all, the house had three bedrooms. One for my mother, a second rented to a married couple helped pay the mortgage, and a third belonged to Connie and me.

That third room stayed empty during the week for almost a year because our roomers and my mother worked all day and leaving her girls alone until she got home from work was never an option for my mother. By then I was in first grade which complicated things even more. Daycare had yet to be invented and, Nanny Retha was the closest thing to it. Momma made just enough to pay her and believed it was a safe choice, even if it wasn't as safe as she imagined, thanks to fat and crazy cousin Donald. Connie and I were in seventh heaven on Fridays when Momma picked us up from the projects to spend the weekend with her at our new house, in a room of our own. We sat ready and waiting in Retha's living room, our coats in our laps and our clothes packed in a little overnight bag. The weekend adventure began with the bus ride across town to South Akron. Being the oldest, I claimed the bus seat next to the window. On winter nights, when it was too dark to see much of anything for most of the trip, I made faces at my own reflection in the glass. But in summer, when the light of day stretched into the evening hours, there was all of Main Street to take in. We passed O'Neil's and Polsky's, the big department stores, Jacobson's—one of the small and pricey specialty shops—and Jordan Marsh, a shoe store also on the expensive end, where we made our annual fall pilgrimage to the kids' floor for new back-to-school shoes. My mother always settled the question of who would be first to stand on the machine that—when Connie or I looked down into it— mysteriously (and maybe even dangerously) let us see the bones of our feet-like parts belonging to little skeletons.

When the bus rolled by Planters Peanuts, we could see the roaster in the store window, where workers cooked peanuts on the spot and dipped them in honey if you wanted something more than plain. And then there was the Palace Theatre with its big marquee and fancy box office. Inside, the ceiling was done up to look like the sky, complete with floating clouds and twinkling stars. Momma once took us there to see Cab Calloway, and as we left the theatre still captivated by the magic of his white tuxedo and tails, slicked back hair, jiving and singing, "Hi-de-hi-de-hi-de-ho," Connie asked, "Momma, can you buy me a man like that?" Momma laughed and replied, "Honey, if they were selling men like that, I'd get me one."

At our stop, we hopped off the bus and walked a three-block stretch to the railroad tracks, crossed them and continued two more blocks and around the corner past the Miami Tavern. Once we passed the bar, with its high windows lit up by neon signs advertising Schlitz beer and Johnnie Walker liquor, we walked another block to our street, Kossuth Court, and to number 124. Even then I thought Court was too grand a word for the narrow, dead-end, roughly paved blacktop and broken cement.

I was seven years old the first time I seriously struggled to claim my independence and demonstrate for my mother that she didn't have to worry about Connie and me while she was at work. At her wit's end, she devised a desperation plan: she and I would leave home together in the mornings, she off to catch a bus to her job at the cleaners and me walking ten or so blocks to Allen Elementary School. Four-year-old Connie would remain at home, with all the doors locked. Stationed on the sectional couch in the living room with a pillow and quilt in case she wanted to nap, and a sandwich and glass of milk on the nearby end table, Connie had strict instructions never to open a door for anyone including me when I came home at lunchtime. From her perch in the living room, my little sister could see me out the window, watching as I ate the sandwich my mother had prepared and neatly wrapped in cellophane that morning, leaving it for me half hidden between the screen and front doors. This latest attempt to have her girls living with her during the week had produced mixed results, especially once fall turned into winter and it was too cold to continue my lunch arrangement.

So now, I was to learn to unlock our big front door and storm door. I was to become a latchkey kid, though that term did not yet exist, at least not for our family. Both my mother and I hoped that once I had mastered the doors, Connie and I could be safe and snug inside the house when my mother came in from work. It would be the final step in Connie and me being freed from Aunt Retha's tyrannical grip and Donald's diabolical fantasies.

On a bitterly cold Sunday afternoon, my mother announced she would begin my door-unlocking lessons. We put on our coats, and I pulled on my cap and mittens. We stepped out onto the front porch, and my mother pulled the door shut behind us. It closed with a heavy thud and the sharp click of the lock. She jiggled the doorknob, making sure the door was locked, and then she firmly closed the double-paned storm door with a push against its aluminum frame.

"You hold the key like this," she said gripping one of the two door keys and pointing the narrow end toward the storm-door lock. Slowly, she inserted the key, gave it a tum and pulled the open door toward us. For the first time, I saw that Connie was watching, standing on the living room couch and looking out the window where she could see Momma and me on the porch.

My mother held up the second key and began demonstrating how to open the main door. "Now with this door, you have to turn the key and push the door—push it hard." She gave the door a shove. It opened, and I felt the warm air from the hallway on my face just for the moment before she slammed the door shut again. Closing the storm door once more, she handed me the ring with the two keys. "Now you try it." I matched the silver-colored key to the storm door. I pointed it, narrow end, grooves up toward the lock and pushed it into the lock and turned the key. The door released. I looked at Connie in the window and broke out into a big grin. "OK, now the big door," I heard my mother say. My fingers felt stiff inside my mittens, and I fumbled slightly with the second key. Holding onto the doorknob, I pulled my body closer to the door and pushed the key toward the lock. Instead of easing into the lock, the key and the ring slipped out of my hand and clattered onto the porch. I quickly picked up the keys and tried again. And again. And again. Each time something went wrong. If I got the key into the lock I couldn't turn it. Or I wasn't strong enough to push the door and turn the key. On my last try, I looked for Connie, but she had stopped watching.

Inside my mittens my fingers were numb. I wanted to get in the house quick and use the toilet. Hot, salty tears rolled down my cold cheeks and comingled with the snot bubbling from my nose. I sucked in a breath to try to stop the tears, but I only succeeded in letting out a deep, strangled gasp like someone fighting for air.

"It's OK, honey," Momma said, patting my head as she smoothly unlocked the big door, gave it a shove and followed me into the warm hallway, closing the door behind her. "Go blow your nose. Where's Connie? You're getting the hang of it. We'll try again tomorrow." We did, and for days after that until I was opening those doors like an old hand and Momma rewarded me with my own set of keys.

Teaching her girls to do things on our own gave my mother great joy. When she wasn't showing us the proper way to iron a blouse, she was instructing us on how to take the bus downtown, where we were to pay certain utility bills with money she carefully portioned out for each debt. (Connie and I quickly learned that if we walked instead of taking the bus, we could use the fare for treats or other fun stuff instead.) And when my mother surprised me on my eighth birthday with a royal blue, two-wheeled Western Flyer bike, she also taught me how to ride it in the dead of winter. I wobbled. I gripped the handlebars. I tried to steer and pedal all at the same time while she walked, then trotted alongside me, a firm hand on the bike seat, her other hand over one of mine on the handlebars. Up and down Miami Street we went, making tire tracks and footprints on the light coating of day-old snow until we were both worn out, me from struggling to stay upright, Momma from working to keep me moving. By the start of the New Year, I was on my own, a graduate of the Susan Tolliver School of Biking. A steady confidence replaced my wobble and uncertainty. I no longer needed my mother's hand on the handlebars, but her coaching mantra, "Keep pedaling, honey, just keep pedaling," never failed me.

Connie and Melba

5—Life in Middle America
Right in the middle of living history.

My colored-girl version of growing up in middle America was happily ordinary. My sister and I did most things together, because my mother insisted, despite my wanting to exercise my supposed big-sister privilege. We collected all the "girl" things. We kept house in a two-story tin doll house. We cut out paper dolls and their wardrobes. We competed in "war" with old decks of cards and bested each other in jacks. We re-played boxing matches between Joe Louis and Billy Cahn, and because I was the big sister, I insisted on being Joe Louis. In our real-life fights with other girls, I tried to outtalk the bullies who pulled my hair, or tore at my clothes taunting, "she thinks she's so cute." Connie, on the other hand, didn't waste words on our enemies. She simply threw punches that landed in their most vulnerable body parts. "Stick together and take up for each other," my mother admonished. "I did, Momma," I reported after one particularly vicious encounter. "I told Connie to run."

When the weather turned warm, we rode our bikes up and down Miami Street and around the neighborhood. In Thornton Park we stood upright on the swings and screamed as we tried going higher and higher. We rooted for Satchel Paige and Larry Doby playing for the Cleveland Indians whether listening to play-by-play announcers on the radio, or in person the special times we actually got to the ballpark with my mother and one of her male friends. And we jumped for joy when the Indians defeated the Boston Red Sox in the 1948 World Series. We ate peanut butter and jelly sandwiches on sliced white Wonder Bread, washed down by ice cold lemonade on hot summer days. In winter, dinner was often meatloaf and sides of pinto beans and hand planted, picked, and canned garden vegetables lining the well-stocked shelves of my mother's fruit cellar. And always, always there was cornbread.

We celebrated the major holidays, usually in Cleveland, with all the aunts, uncles, and cousins. Sometimes they came to our house in Akron and my mother laid out the spread even when we didn't have a separate dining room, and folks made do with trays.

The grownups began marking their calendars when the big holidays, especially Thanksgiving and Christmas, got close. It meant they needed to get busy. Aunt Clarice would shortly be headed our way, boarding a Cleveland-bound train at New York City's Penn Station. And for those siblings who might host her, it was time to get out the best towels and washcloths, the carnation-scented bars of soap still wrapped in tissue—bath item gifts from their elder sister that they in turn saved for special occasions like her visits. The best bed linens got pulled out of closets and cedar chests. Windows got a thorough cleaning with vinegar, water, and newspapers. All the special china and glasses were treated to their annual hand washing and drying.

At our house, where most of the walls were papered, my mother handed us a light blue cleaner resembling playdough, gave Connie and me our own tennis ball-sized clumps of the stuff and demonstrated how we should rid the walls of scuff marks with our oversized wallpaper cleaners. In other words make the walls look like new—or as close to new as possible. "Be sure to get into those corners," she instructed us after we finished the walls and moved on to giving the woodwork a Spic and Span scrub. "And don't spare the elbow grease. You know Clarice will be expecting every inch of the house to be spotless."

No matter who of my mother's sisters and brothers hosted the holiday dinner, the set up was the same, adults at a big dining table covered with platters of food, and kids seated at one or two small tables and low chairs removed from the grownups and their conversations, but within range of the adult eyes. At the adult table things usually started out quietly, everyone acting polite, as they carved the turkey and passed the ham. But you could count on it that halfway through the meal, the grownups grew more animated, usually with Clarice reminding her younger siblings of what their home life was like growing up in Cave Spring. "None of you are old enough to remember, but I picked cotton to earn money to go away to school," Clarice would say.

She had earned a teaching certificate in Alabama and returned home to teach at a local colored-school near where the Turners lived. "And Poppa always held back some of my pay, so it took me longer than it should have to save up my tuition." Despite her father's insistence that she stay in Georgia and teach, Clarice defiantly squirreled away money for nursing school in New York.

When remembering their father, Clarice and her sisters and brothers all agreed on two things: Dallas Coates Turner considered his family superior to their neighbors, and he ruled his own household with an iron hand. So, when Clarice claimed that their father had paid himself some of her cotton-picking money, nobody doubted that she spoke the truth. Tensions rose and arguments erupted whenever the siblings' talk turned to the amount and frequency of Clarice's largesse after she finished nursing school, got established in New York, and began sending money back home. It had been Clarice's money that helped pay for the boarding-school education of four younger members of the Turner family.

"I left home not long after Clarice," insisted Dallas, oldest of the surviving three brothers. "So, I never looked to her for help." Before he could go on, Albert chimed in, "You're wrong Dallas. You were still in the house when...." Before Albert could finish, Geraldine, youngest of the five Turner sisters, interrupted with, "Well, me, Sue, Clyde, and Al all have nobody but Clarice to thank for giving us the chance to go to Barber," Barber being the Presbyterian boarding school in neighboring Anniston, Alabama where she, my mother, and their two younger brothers went away from home to go to high school.

By the time the dinner plates and silver were collected and the assorted desserts of pineapple upside-down cake, vanilla ice cream, pumpkin pie and fruitcake were set out, Dallas would be tipsy and mad at everybody. Clyde would be arguing that Clarice had promised him a watch, a graduation gift he said he never got. "You start this every year, Clyde," my Aunt Rovena would scold. "You're grown. Buy your own self a watch if you want one."

My mother would sit at one corner of the dining table, an ashtray in front of her, a Camel cigarette poised between two fingers of one hand and a cup of cream and sugared coffee within easy reach of the other hand for whenever she decided to have a sip. "Sue, you make the best pineapple upside-down cake," Clarice would say as she cut herself a second healthy slice. "Momma teach you to bake? Or Poppa?" Their father had supported the family as a cook at the nearby school for the deaf and dumb. My mother would answer with a smile, "They both did," and let her brothers and sisters continue their squabbling.

It fell to my cousins, my sister, and me to provide some of the lighter moments of these family gatherings. "Show us some of the latest dance steps," was all the adults had to say to get us kids up and performing "the Hucklebuck," or "the Camelwalk." We all got into the act and competed furiously, showing off our steps to the point where sweat rolled off our faces and onto our holiday outfits. "Now that's enough," my mother would say firmly to end our performances. "Melba and Connie, have a seat."

Television came late to the Tolliver household. When it did finally arrive in 1952, we welcomed our big boxy Dumont with a room of its own. The space had originally been our back porch. My mother, in one of her renovating moods, thought the space could be put to better use and she enlisted my uncle Clyde to box in the porch and panel it with golden knotty pine. In the new TV room, Connie and I would pull our chairs up so close to the Dumont's five-inch screen that our noses practically touched it. There, in the dark, as if in a movie theatre, we watched whatever happened to be on, sometimes watching the test pattern before we learned better.

TV became a door through which we welcomed a parade of strangers: Ed Sullivan, Steve Allen, Dagmar, Howdy Doody, Molly Goldberg, all bringing their worlds into ours.

Through that same door came people we felt some kin to: Nat "King" Cole, Billy Eckstine, Sarah Vaughan, and "Sugar" Ray Robinson, even Amos 'n' Andy.

My mother paid good money for that TV even though she didn't buy it at a department store. The TV was a castoff from Aunt Rovena, Momma's older hairdresser sister who was looking to clear some space in her own living room for a new model.

Trading up in the world—whether in people or things— pleased my Aunt Rovena. A smart and successful businesswoman, she had converted the front entry of her house into a cozily efficient beauty shop. If we knew nothing about Rovena there was evidence of two things that could not be denied. She could fix hair, and she could make money. Between Rovena's sales pitch and my mother's bargaining skill, the two sisters struck a deal and the Tollivers marched into the television age with the rest of the world.

The second-hand nature of our TV didn't bother Connie and me, but when word spread in the family that Rovena had *sold* it to my mother and not given it to her, my Uncle Albert, their elegant, pipe-smoking, dental-entrepreneur brother coolly instructed, "Sue, I want you to go downtown today and pick out any TV you want, and I'll pay for it."

The day the new TV arrived, the department store delivery men carefully unloaded the giant packing box, slowly carried the precious cargo up the steps, onto the front porch and into the front hallway with Connie and me acting as the forward guard, making sure the movers had a clear path through the living and dining rooms, into the knotty pine room. There they set down a new Magnavox in the spot recently vacated by the old Dumont.

On winter evenings after dinner, after the leftovers were put away and the dishes washed and dried, my mother set aside her sewing, and for an hour or so the three of us piled onto the little sofa and watched our favorite shows. If it happened to be wintertime, when temperatures in the unheated back room dipped ten degrees lower than the rest of the house, we bundled up under an old wool patchwork quilt to ward off the chill.

Much as we got a kick out of watching TV's limited fare, the tube barely altered our news-consuming habits. We still listened to WAKR radio. We still got the *Akron Beacon Journal* delivered on Sunday and picked up the local Black weekly on Saturday. If something caught my mother's eye in the supermarket ads, like a special on hamburger at Kroger's, she noted it: "Remind me when we go shopping on Saturday. I'll pick up some and make you guys some chili." Or if she recognized a name in the obituary pages, she read the item aloud to Connie and me, with commentary: "Mmm-mm-mm, Mr. Johnson passed. His funeral isat Mount Olive. He was just fifty-six." My mother considered news to be anything bearing on our everyday lives. And if she came across an article meeting that standard, she read it out loud to us, often between puffs of one of her unfiltered Camel cigarettes. She was our up close and personal news anchor with the unquestioned authority and attitude to be convincing.

TV couldn't hold a candle to the Cleveland radio station that Connie and I and our best girlfriends listened to every Saturday at midnight. Sprawled across the floor of our bedroom or on our bunk beds in our flannel pajamas, we tuned in to Alan "Moondog" Freed. A Jewish DJ who sounded Blacker than any white man we knew, Freed played the music of Black R&B performers when most white DJs wouldn't—everyone from Big Maybelle to Big Mamma Thornton, and Chuck Berry to The Platters. We especially loved it when Moondog announced his listeners' song requests, phoned in ahead of time. If one of ours made it on the air, Freed would say, "Now, Melba in Akron wants us to play, 'In the Still of the Night' and dedicate it to her boyfriend, Deanie." Hooo! Hearing our names over the radio, and our boyfriends' names, too, with some of our other girlfriends probably listening in their own bedrooms! Boy oh boy, it was thrilling, a high that lasted for weeks.

A large part of my growing up years happened in the summers, in New York City, visiting my Aunt Clarice.

Clarice had come up from Cave Spring, Georgia to do her nurse's training in New York and never left. She loved nothing more than showing New York to her country kinfolks. All her sisters and brothers visited Clarice at one time or another, including my mother who never took time off from work, unless forced to because the cleaners that employed her shut down. She treated herself to no more than a couple of real vacations in her entire lifetime. But she regaled Connie and me with stories about Smalls Paradise and Sugar Ray's, celebrated nightclubs on Seventh Avenue in Harlem, that she had gone to with friends on one New York visit.

When kids in the family were old enough to travel alone on the bus or train, and our public schools let out for the summer, Clarice would treat Connie and me, and our Cleveland cousins—Aunt Rovena's two girls, Janice and Diane, and Uncle Albert's son, Michael—to a week in the big city. In preparation for our visits, she childproofed her best furniture—piano, mahogany headboards and other bedroom furniture—with crisp white sheets as protection against possible scrapes by her guests.

From year to year, Clarice's list of must-see tourist sites never varied: we rode the double-decker buses on Fifth Avenue, watched the Rockettes at Radio City Music Hall, and live performances at the Roxy Theatre, slid our change into the automat at Horn & Hardart. As the coins cascaded and levers turned, slots dropped behind windows to open for our choices of chicken salad sandwiches and slices of apple pie. We climbed the stairs of the Statue of Liberty, walked all over Coney Island eating Nathan's hot dogs, and peered through the bars of the Central Park Zoo wondering how the heck animals out of Africa made it all the way to New York City. At Macy's, we bought small treasures to take back home to our mothers: a music box, a bottle of cologne, an Aunt Jemima cookie jar. And we sent postcards to our folks back home.

We cousins thought we were showing good manners when we once invited Clarice to come back to Ohio with us. "What? Follow you guys home? Never!" Family members still laugh about Clarice's instant reply, a family joke that folks never tire of repeating.

As an adult, I learned that the Dunbar Apartments, in central Harlem between 149th and 150th Streets, and 7th and 8th Avenues, the very place Clarice called home, deserved its own spot on her list of remarkable places. Her two-bedroom apartment was right in the middle of living history. Named for the poet, Paul Lawrence Dunbar, and built by the Rockefellers, the Dunbar was the first housing complex of its kind and an award-winning example of elegance and utility. Construction of the Dunbar had added much-needed housing for the rapidly increasing population of Black Harlemites. Its residents included everyday folks like my aunt who'd come to New York during the Great Migration and stayed on, working their way into the city's Black middle class. The list of the day's movers and shakers who also lived there included A. Philip Randolph, stately founder of the first Black trade union, the Brotherhood of Sleeping Car Porters; Bill "Bojangles" Robinson, the master of tap dancing; E. Sims Campbell, cartoonist and illustrator for major weekly magazines including *Saturday Evening Post*; actor Leigh Whipper; bandleader Fletcher Henderson; and W.E.B. Dubois, the writer and civil rights activist. Paul Robeson, the great international singer and outspoken government critic, also lived there for a time with his wife, Essie. The *Dunbar News,* a bulletin, kept residents abreast of the goings on in their enclave.

The Dunbar, and the folks who lived there, were nowhere to be found in the schools and the books where, as an impressionable young colored girl, I was learning America's history. Even so, whether celebrated and high-profile people, or ordinary, everyday folks, the Dunbar residents were change-makers shaping American culture, politics, and social movements.

In 1952, between my freshman and sophomore years at South High School, the Republicans nominated Dwight Eisenhower for president. Neither the GOP's convention—the first to be televised—nor their "I Like Ike" slogan got much traction in my South Akron neighborhood. Nobody sported buttons broadcasting their political leanings. And the significance of Betty Furness making history during that convention, opening and closing the door of a Westinghouse refrigerator while selling its virtues on live TV, was lost on me. I had no idea that the twenty-eight wardrobe changes she made were her own clothes, that she rejected sponsor suggestions of aprons, and did her own hair to assure sole control of her on-camera image.

I was a lot older when I met Betty and got to know her. We would later work together at WNBC-TV in New York, and I would interview her for a profile piece in *USA Today*.

With Eisenhower's inauguration early the next year—also a *first* for live TV—I got a taste of the global village. That's not what our tenth-grade civics teacher called it when our school set up a TV in our classroom and gathered us around it. But she did remind us that people all across the country were watching an event as it was happening, and that would be true of people all around the world within our lifetimes.

In those early days of TV, Dorothy Fuldheim of WEWS in Cleveland was the lone woman reporting the happenings in Northeast Ohio or hosting one of the station's public affairs programs. That she was a woman, didn't impress me as much as how ancient she seemed to my fourteen-year-old eyes.

For girls growing up in Akron—or in most of America during the 1940's and 50's, TV reporting—despite Fuldheim—was not in the picture when thinking about their life choices after high school. If, instead of getting married and starting a family, a girl wanted a career, she generally had three options: nurse, teacher, or social worker.

I considered none of those. I secretly dreamed of becoming an acclaimed ballerina, or a movie star like the brown and beautiful Dorothy Dandridge who radiated glamour and drove poor Harry Belafonte crazy in *Carmen Jones*. Meantime, my mother had other ideas.

6—Words Matter

"You have a good mind when you use it."

When my mother divorced my father and her role changed from wife to single mother and head of household, nobody we knew ever said or even thought my sister and I came from "a broken home." The home my mother made for herself and Connie and me in Kossuth Court was whole and holy. And homeschooling—even if I had heard the word, which I never did—would have held a different meaning for my mother and all the other folks that had a hand in raising my sister and me. Home was where my mother—our first teacher—schooled us in how to be in the world. And her most repeated words of instruction—not limited to bike riding—were to trust her and ourselves, and to keep going, keep moving.

I once read somewhere that parents are authors of our childhood, and after that we write our own stories.

In creating the narrative of my childhood—done by instinct or intuition—my parents—especially my mother—exercised their agency over language and chose to ignore or outright reject vocabulary that portrayed people like us as inferior, incompetent, or incapable. They understood the language intended to exploit and manipulate—and when all else failed—to make people like us invisible. The language of exclusion and derision underpinning American-style apartheid my parents experienced full-time "down South," and all too often "up North," was mostly deleted from my childhood story.

In that story we were never "underprivileged." Lods Street and Kossuth Court where we lived in Akron were not "hoods," or "ghettos." They were neighborhoods, places where people like us lived. My parents worked hard at jobs. Not careers. They never made a lot of money. And they were sometimes "broke," but never "poor," or "poverty-stricken." We were never "minorities." We were nobody's "diverse." Neither were we subject to any of the linguistic inventions concocted by those who, in later years, would use their social science and their majority status to distinguish themselves from us without exposing their own biases and intentions. In other words, "to keep those people in their place."

My folks said I was colored. Not Black. Not Afro-American. Not African American. Not "people of color."

I grew up hearing a bad-behaving person called a "negro," if the speaker was my dignified Uncle Albert expressing his disgust with someone. And bad-acting folks were labeled "nigger" before the label was amputated to "the 'n' word."

When talking about my sister and me, "My rabbits" was a favorite expression of my mother's. "Honey" often book-ended the conversations she had with us. And almost everyone close to us ran "MelbaandConnie" together as if naming one instead of two brown-skinned girls with neatly parted hair, braided in three plaits, and sporting dresses homemade by a loving mother.

"Showing out" or "talking back" by her rabbits was something my mother didn't take kindly to, it crossed a line and drew a certain look from her, followed, if need be, by instructions to "Go get my belt." Those words told us all we needed to know of her belief in the words, "spare the rod and spoil the child."

Our homeschooling also instilled in us the belief that to succeed in the larger America, the America of white supremacy, in which racism was embedded, we had to be "twice as smart" and work "twice as hard" as our white contemporaries.

That was not to say that we were taught to hate white people. My mother worked in their cleaners. She shopped in their stores, including a couple in the neighborhood. She sometimes bought her Camel cigarettes, or a few cents worth of lunch meat, in Watson's, a tiny crammed-full grocery run by a white family with West Virginia roots, or at Balogh's, also just down the block and owned by a sister and brother whose family came from somewhere in Eastern Europe.

As young children, the names we had for white people— "ofays" and "honkies" (probably a shortened version of Hungarian)—were words we picked up from our peers and never used at home simply because my mother wouldn't have put up with those words and because white people were rarely the subjects of our childhood conversations.

Connie and I had been well-fortified and inoculated by language and life by the time my mother sent us off to public school. The difference between my schooling at home and in the public system was striking, and I would never again—not in elementary or high school—have another Black teacher. It was just accepted that regardless of the complexion of the student body, there were only one or two colored teachers in the entire Akron public school system.

Not that the white teachers were uniformly uncaring or ignorant of my world. I remember in particular, my fifth-grade teacher, Mrs. Lewis, and how she and I made a couple of awkward adjustments as we—on occasion—traded roles as teacher and student.

I liked Mrs. Lewis a lot and believed there was a good story to explain why she had a wooden leg. When she walked from her desk to the blackboard, or down the rows of student desks, her steps made a unique sound: one step, a pause, and a thump, one step, a pause, and a thump. She never spoke about her missing leg, or if the wooden leg and foot gave her problems when she bought shoes. I had so many questions about Mrs. Lewis, but I knew to keep them to myself. In the year I spent in her classroom, Mrs. Lewis never explained herself and simply allowed her students' curiosity to evaporate into the classroom air along with the chalk dust, the smell of rubber erasers, and the scratches of our number six lead pencils on paper.

For no good reason—maybe it was my prior homeschooling—I got the idea that while Mrs. Lewis never asked me about myself, she just might like to know more about me. So, on the day that a classroom discussion turned to the subject of hair I told Mrs. Lewis and the rest of the class that my mother washed my hair with Tide, the same laundry detergent she used to clean our family's clothes, bed linens, and towels. Mrs. Lewis's jaw dropped in disbelief before she recovered and quickly remarked, "Melba. Your hair is so beautiful. You must get your mother to write the Tide company and tell them about her new use for their product. I'm sure they'd be happy to know about it." Telling Mrs. Lewis the rest of the story, the part about my hair turning nappy once it was wet and my mother spending a couple of hours straightening it out with a hot comb, seemed unfair, like it would spoil the picture Mrs. Lewis had in her head about my hair. But the other Black kids in the class knew that I was holding out on Mrs. Lewis, and that when it came to our hair, she was still in the dark.

Another time, a comment from Mrs. Lewis in response to something I said left me wondering where knowledge is lodged within us human beings and if we come into the world already knowing all there is to know. Mrs. Lewis had us read something aloud and then posed a question about it. I raised my hand and when she called on me, I gave an answer, without prompting, that seemed to be already inside me, just waiting to be shared. Mrs. Lewis was pleased and said, "Melba, you have a good mind (pause), when you use it." But I could tell she didn't know that I hadn't *thought* about the answer or exerted any effort to find it, hadn't consciously called upon my mind. The answer was just there. In succeeding years, in other situations, I have thought of Mrs. Lewis whenever I experience this already-known knowledge that scholars and researchers call *spontaneous knowledge*. And each time, I find the experience just as unexpected, just as mysterious and full of wonder as when I was in the fifth grade.

7—I Can Do That
Splits, Kicks, and Cartwheels

Algebra. Oof. Just the word itself made me wish I were back in the eighth grade instead of starting my first day of high school. I knew my way around Allen Elementary. I knew the teachers and all the kids in my class and even some in the lower grades with my sister and her friends. Now, here I stood outside a closed door checking and double checking my class assignment card. My teacher was supposed to be a Mr. Kuntz. Could he have already started the class? I reached for the doorknob and opened the door just wide enough to confirm my worst thoughts. A man in a dark suit stood at the teacher's desk. Before I could push the door closed, he turned away from his student audience and looked squarely at me. I quickly shut the door and leaned against it, my heart beating much too fast. I took a deep breath. Should I go to the principal's office and ask somebody there to help me find my algebra class? Or just stay out in the hallway and wait for the bell signaling class change? Or take yet another look behind the closed door? Three choices and I didn't want any of them. I took another deep breath and reached again for the doorknob. When I opened the door this time, the man in the dark suit who really was Mr. Kuntz, said sternly, "Make up your mind.

Come in or stay out." Pretending I didn't hear the kids who giggled and turned to follow me with their eyes, I headed for an empty desk at the back of the room before Mr. Kuntz told my agitators to stop watching me and pay attention to him.

That first year as I sized up my situation it seemed to me that the coolest girls in the school were the cheerleaders and I wanted to be one of them. I pictured myself wearing the royal blue uniform, the black-and-white saddle shoes, and the fluffy angora-topped bobbysocks. I didn't sit down and think, "This is odd. I'm here in a school where colored kids make up most of the student body, there are ten cheerleaders, and none of them are colored. Not now, not ever in the whole history of the school. And for that matter, no colored girl has ever been a drum majorette either."

That a line had been drawn between colored girls like me and my cheerleading dreams, a line I should not try to cross, never entered my mind. It didn't occur to me that I shouldn't try to become a member of the cheerleading squad (or the special gym team, or the girl's athletic letter club, for that matter) just because no one like me had ever been chosen before. So, when tryouts were announced in my freshman year to choose the junior varsity team, I made it my business to show up. Watching other girls do splits and cartwheels in practice, I thought, "I can do that." It was the older cheerleaders, the ones moving up to the varsity team that showed us the routines. They were sure of themselves, confident and friendly with each other. I watched them and waited my turn to show what I could do. I wasn't nervous or afraid. Just the opposite, I felt equal to and in some cases even superior to the other girls when it came to performing the routines. I was even confident in my looks, even if I wasn't blonde or freckled. I guess I thought I was pretty cute, based on my own beauty standards. I was a Noxzema girl and had made it a daily ritual to slather my face with the strong-smelling white stuff in the dark blue jar. Plus a few boys had told me that I had pretty legs. Legs were very important in those days, especially since the twin bumps on my chest barely qualified as real breasts. There was also the time in the girls' bathroom that a blonde, white girl told me out of the blue that she thought I was very pretty. She was a majorette. And while she didn't have the best reputation— and other girls bad-mouthed her behind her back—I was flattered by the unexpected compliment from a girl so unlike me, whom I considered the most glamorous female in the school.

With each round of cheerleader eliminations, I found myself still in the running and my confidence soared.

But then a strange thing happened. Just as I saw my goal within reach and I would be picked for the junior squad, I got cold feet. I was afraid. My fears had nothing to do with my ability to turn cartwheels, jump high or perform splits. I began to worry about adding to my mother's financial burden. I worried she wouldn't have money for all of the cheerleading paraphernalia: angora socks, new black-and-white saddle shoes, specially-made uniforms, and who knows what else. I worried she might have to work overtime, to take in extra sewing, to pay for everything. And how would I get to the out-of-town football and basketball games? We had no car. On and on, my worries piled up until they threatened to smother me. At one point, I had my mother losing our house over a pair of angora bobbysocks. I knew my dream would put a serious strain on my mother's meager income.

On the day before the new team was to be announced, I went home for lunch as usual and when I finished my sandwich I got up from the kitchen table, walked out into the hallway, and there, by myself, in the deadly silence I got down on my knees in the stairway and had a long talk with God, asking Him and His son Jesus to not let me get picked for cheerleader. I prayed with everything in me, "God, dear God, please, please don't let them choose me. Please, please." The next morning, I sat in French class and crossed my fingers when the PA system came on and the principal announced the names of the new cheerleaders. Mine wasn't one of them. My prayers had been answered.

The next year was a different story. When cheerleader try-outs rolled around, I showed up again, and again I believed I was good enough to be chosen. Although our family fortunes hadn't changed, for reasons I couldn't explain, I felt confident that if I made the team, the money would come. I did and it did.

The new cheerleaders' names were announced from the principal's office over the public address system during my French class with Miss Van Dis. A white woman and one of the homeliest-looking people I'd ever seen, and awkward as a newborn pony, Miss Van Dis topped my list of favorite teachers. I felt a deep, unusual kindness half hidden behind her classroom reserve. Her buck-toothed smile and the look in her eyes behind her horn-rimmed glasses as the announcer called my name told me that she was proud and happy for me.

The opposite of Miss Van Dis was Miss Higgins, the girls' gym teacher. I never felt good about her. She offered me no support or good wishes even after I made the team. And I could not imagine that she put in a good word for me when she and the other teachers were deciding who would be the new cheerleaders. Besides having a say about cheerleaders, Miss Higgins had sole discretion over which girls got selected for her two other organizations, "S" Club, the girls' version of the boys' athletic letter club, and Special Gym, the much admired, high-level gymnastic group for girls. No colored girls were ever chosen for either of them. And it looked to me like as long as Miss Higgins—with her short steel-gray hair tucked behind her ears, her white short-sleeve shirt and black cotton shorts that bloused just below the butt—was in charge, she would not be inclined to change those whites-only programs.

My third year at South High School, Joan Threat, a senior student, Black as the ace of spades, with a winning smile and personality to match was named Homecoming Queen. A first. And as I remember, a choice made by student vote. In the period after the announcement, I rushed to gym class, breathless with the news. I approached Miss Higgins with, "Isn't it great? Joan is Homecoming Queen!" Miss Higgins shot me an icy stare through silver-rimmed glasses, and without a word turned and walked away, her back ramrod straight. The message was clear: "No it is not great. Joan, and by extension none of you colored girls, are good enough." When I learned that Joan chose to continue her education after high school at Fisk University, the Black, all-girls college in Tennessee that I had never heard of, I decided I wanted to go there, too.

8—Goodbye Akron, Hello Fifth Avenue

"You'll always have a job."

Both my mother and her sister believed that nursing had allowed my Aunt Clarice to carve out a comfortable middle-class life for herself, and both women thought it would do the same for me. "You'll always have a job," my mother reasoned.

Besides steady employment, a nursing education appealed to my mother because she had no college tuition money set aside for me, and I hadn't applied for any scholarships.

My South High homeroom teacher and guidance counselor had shown little interest in helping me figure out my future, except to say on more than one occasion and to more than one female student, "It's as easy to marry a rich man as a poor one." Far as we students knew this guidance counselor was never married, and how she acquired much less believed this bit of wisdom was a mystery.

Clarice's suggestion that I apply to the Bellevue School of Nursing made all the sense in the world to my mother. Bellevue was in New York City where Clarice lived, and she would be only too happy to keep an eye on me in the big city.

Neither my mother nor I knew the first thing about the Bellevue School of Nursing, but after Clarice's recommendation, my mother only needed to hear that she could handle the first year's tuition of two-hundred-thirty-nine dollars. Plus, thanks to a committee of philanthropic, white society ladies, students received a twenty-dollar monthly stipend. Ten dollars the students got to keep, a handsome sum back then considering that twenty-five cents bought a milkshake or a malted. The other ten bucks went into an account to pay for books, shoes, and other necessities. Bellevue picked up the tuition tab for the second and third years of the students' training.

The thought of leaving home to spend three years at Bellevue held no appeal for me, but my best friend, Martha Starks, loved the idea and was dying to be a nurse. Martha had graduated high school a year ahead of me and when I told her about Bellevue we made a pact: she agreed to wait a year so that we could apply to Bellevue at the same time, just the way we did everything together. When she got white buck oxford shoes, I begged my mother to get me a pair. My sister Connie and I tagged along with Martha's family to Sunday school and church at Mt. Olive Baptist. When Martha got baptized, I followed her a few months later, holding my breath when Reverand Monroe dipped me into the chilly water and pronounced me saved.

Martha and I talked about boyfriends and clothes and hairstyles. We shared secrets about the girls who "did it," and reported the news flash of having started our periods. Martha and I walked to South High together every morning—up the wrought iron stairs rising three stories to the concrete bridge, making a left to hike the mile-and-a-half to school.

In her junior year, everything changed. Her family moved away from South Akron. I couldn't get over her parents doing that. The Starks family had bought a house in a supposedly better neighborhood on the West Side, in a mostly white and Jewish part of town.

Now Martha would go to Buchtel High, where they offered students trigonometry and three years of a language, compared to South High's more limited scholastic menu: college prep or not, math up through geometry, and only two years of a foreign language. Buchtel fielded lousy football teams. They had great classes but couldn't throw passes. Sports teams mattered at South High and the glass cases in the hallways filled with football and basketball trophies proved it, even if most South High students would end their education after the twelfth grade.

After Martha graduated, she got a job in a dentist's office while we continued making our Bellevue plans. As the application deadline neared, I completed the paperwork and sent it off in the mail. I imagined it landing on a desk at Bellevue where a pair of eyes would look it over and decide to make me part of the Fall 1959 class. Martha mailed her application the same day. Then we waited. And we waited. The waiting ended with Bellevue spoiling our plans. They accepted me and rejected Martha.

The eyes reading the applications didn't understand. Martha was the much better student. She would make a great nurse. It wasn't right. It wasn't fair. Once Martha and I got over our shock and disappointment, we figured the rejection came down to class standing in our respective graduation classes. At Martha's *better* school, she had just missed being in the top ten percent. And I, at the not-so-great school, had had an easier time in making it into that group.

But Martha or no Martha, no way was my mother allowing me to back out of Bellevue.

So, in June, a week after returning my rented graduation cap and gown, and my diploma safely tucked away, Momma took me downtown to the Greyhound bus station, handed over the money for my one-way ticket to New York City, and kept an eye on the bus driver as he loaded my big suitcase in the luggage compartment. Her graduation gift to me, an apple-green portable Singer sewing machine, rode in the seat next to me. For a second time in my mother's life and mine, she engaged in a loving, hard labor, pushing me out of my comfortable home and into a bigger world. This time, I was not wearing my birthday suit, but sporting a going-away outfit made with her own caring hands. I wore an oatmeal-colored, wool tweed suit, its three-quarter length coat carefully lined with a silky fabric patterned in delicate swirls that matched my short-sleeved blouse. I felt very grown up.

Waiting for me at the end of the eight-hour bus trip was a bedroom in my aunt's place in the Dunbar, scene of those summer vacation visits with my cousins. In no time I had a summer job at Lord & Taylor's department store on Fifth Avenue, thanks to Miss Wiggins, my aunt's good friend and her former nursing school classmate.

My aunt and her female friends, especially her Lincoln classmates, for reasons I never understood, always called each other "Miss" so and so, or by just their last names. And Miss Wiggins, who had gotten herself kicked out of nursing school for what my aunt described as a minor infraction, had worked at Lord & Taylor for many years as a clerk in the buyer's office for children's clothes. When Miss Wiggins recommended me for a summer job in the same office sorting little tags for kids' clothing at the main store as well as Bala Cynwyd and other ritzy towns I had never heard of, I got the job, no questions asked. I was impressed that Miss Wiggins had that kind of pull. Thanks to her, I learned the important lesson that being in the right place at the right time—and having the right people know you—counted almost as much as experience, in landing a job.

Whenever Clarice reminisced about her nursing-school days at Lincoln Hospital, she painted a picture of long days, hard work, and strict rules and regulations. And when she retold the story of how the school had dismissed Miss Wiggins a year short of graduation, sadness crept into my aunt's voice and regret into her eyes, as if the memory of a perceived wrong done to someone who became a lifelong friend was still fresh in her mind.

Just weeks out of high school I had landed my first job. And I was changing, evolving into a different person. And at the end of every week, I had earned about a third of what my mother earned at the dry cleaners, and this money was all mine. Plus, I dressed up every day complete with stockings and high heels, and I took the bus downtown to mid-Manhattan on my own.

Bellevue and nursing were looking less attractive by the day. I hoped that somehow, while I still had the Lord & Taylor job, the school would notify me that my acceptance was a big mistake. But in September, my place was still waiting for me.

School started on September 17th, 1956, my best friend Martha's nineteenth birthday.

9—Bellevue Probie to RN

"You're the cream of the crop."

Bellevue opened its nursing school in Manhattan on a trial basis in 1873 to train six white students. The school was still exercising its "whites only" policy more than six decades later, around the time I was born, and the school turned down my Aunt Clarice when she applied to be a student there. She was steered instead to Lincoln Hospital in the Bronx. New York City ran both hospitals and their nurses training programs. But Lincoln's school, founded in 1898, was exclusively for the preparation of colored nurses.

Clarice rarely complained about this or let on to others that the New York City of her imagination, the city that she had struggled mightily to migrate to, the progressive, liberal bastion of the North had people in power who practiced some of the same racist policies that stymied blacks trying to move up in the world back home in Cave Spring, Georgia.

The paradox may have surprised or disappointed, but it could not have escaped her.

Tenacity drove my aunt to keep going against the odds and that quality extended well beyond earning a registered nurse's license. Anytime she believed her way of doing things made most sense—and that was most of the time—and if she had set her sights on a clear goal, watch out.

Nobody understood this better than her eight surviving younger brothers and sisters, my mother included.

In September 1956, a generation since my aunt's rejection, I am being welcomed to Bellevue. Me, a sho-nuff, clearly-colored girl. I am one of a-hundred-ninety incoming freshmen, the largest nursing class in history. Most of us are recent high school grads, American-born and largely from the New York area. We are mostly women, but half a dozen men, some of whom served in the military, comprise the Mills School, the small male contingent of the Bellevue Schools of Nursing.

I know little of this and none of it matters to me anyhow on this early autumn afternoon. I'm feeling out of place and out of sorts, in no mood for this first meeting of new students filling the seats of the big auditorium where the school's top brass is already seated onstage. I am feeling sorry for myself. I want to be back home in the comfort of Kossuth Court with Momma and Connie, enjoying being a teenager and looking forward to roller skating at Summit Beach on Tuesday nights or showing off my latest dance steps at one of the Saturday night high school mixers. And if I couldn't be back in Akron, I think I would still be happy holding down my short-lived job at Lord & Taylor, drawing a weekly paycheck just like a grownup.

Despite my funk, instinct leads me to grab a seat not in one of the front rows, but close enough to the stage where I can get a good look at my superiors. I want to see everything, yet not be noticed by the formidable lineup of middle-aged white women on stage whom I will be answering to for the next three years.

A couple of them wear civilian clothes. The rest are in crisp white nurses' uniforms, white shoes, and stockings.

They sit primly, ankles crossed, hair perfectly coifed. They also wear distinctly different caps. Anyone interested in such things, can tell from each nurse's cap where she went to school. This audience naturally directs most of its attention to the Bellevue cap resting crown-like on some of the onstage bigwigs' heads.

Reminiscent of a bakery confection because of its light weight and ruffled edging, the Bellevue cap has earned the affectionate moniker, "organdy cupcake." In spite of its deceptively fragile appearance, the Bellevue cap signifies to the hard-nosed medical world that the nurses who wear it have survived a rigorous training, one that many consider the nursing equivalent of Parris Island, the Marine boot camp.

I'm still refusing to be cheered up when in the course of this welcome-to-Bellevue session, one speaker reminds us that nursing is a caring profession. She also notes that belonging to a union is not one of the profession's many attributes. Kind of like organized labor is below the dignity of nurses. Then, sounding the final congratulatory note, Miss Thelma Ryan takes her turn at the podium, looks out on our sea of upturned faces, and announces, "You are the cream of the crop."

So, today I am "the cream of the crop," but if I had tried to get into Bellevue just thirteen years earlier, in 1943 when the school dropped its restrictive acceptance policy, I would have been part of the "need not apply" crowd.

No one speaking at that welcome meeting notes this turnaround or applauds the young women on whose shoulders I am standing, young women no less intelligent than me, no less deserving than me, and possibly more committed to caring for the sick than me, but who were turned away because of their skin color. Those young colored women had more than paid my dues. And the pity of it is that I would never even know their names. With one exception: my Aunt Clarice.

To my youthful way of thinking, hospitals, like doctors' and dentists' offices, were places to be avoided except in cases of extreme emergencies. Never a candy striper or any other kind of hospital volunteer, I had only my experiences as a patient in two short stays at Akron General and Children's Hospital to form my ideas about the places and the people who cared for the ill and injured. In eighth grade I had surgery to repair a hernia, an experience that left me with one clear memory: A masked man—the anesthetist— instructing me to start counting backwards from one hundred just before he released sweet smelling ether into the apparatus covering my nose, sending me into another world. I had a second surgery my sophomore year of high school to remove a benign breast lump and except for a scar on my right breast, nothing from that visit left a lasting impression on me.

No wonder then that my experiences at Akron's biggest and best hospitals bore not even the slightest resemblance to Bellevue, America's oldest, and a city unto itself, a hulking sprawl of dark red brick spread over four square blocks between Manhattan's First Avenue and the East River. The first time I laid eyes on Bellevue, I wanted to run, it looked so ominous and forbidding, even in daylight, especially as it hovered over the brand-new nurses' residence and school next door. The new residence, built in a 1950's modern style with light-colored tiles and many windows, is always referred to as "440," its address on East 26th Street, and the last building before you run into the FDR Drive and the East River. The location made for great views from the school's upper floors.

The classrooms, library, gym and swimming pool, dining room, auditorium, mailroom, and lounge occupied the lower floors. And then there were the beau parlors.

Some thoughtful soul foresaw the possibility that if the Bellevue nurses' residence was to be a home away from home for young women, then it should include a place for them to meet with their male friends. With that in mind, the residence design incorporated some not-too-public, not-too-private spaces reminiscent in name and in fact of the Victorian era. Called beau parlors and a little bigger than a medium-sized closet, they had enough space for a couple of chairs, a lamp, a table, all laid out within shouting distance of the main floor entrance. The parlors had no doors, and a sheet of speckled glass forming one wall gave the appearance if not the reality of minimal privacy. Visitors to the beau parlors passed through the school's main entrance, and checked in with Miss Byron, the nurse who commanded the front desk. An impressive major domo figure decked out in white uniform and Bellevue cap, with an ever present, extravagantly embroidered handkerchief pinned to her amble bust, she made sure that under her watch, beau parlors remained hanky-panky free zones. And of course, the dormitory floors were strictly off limits to male guests.

Technically, our male classmates had their own Mills School for men pursuing nursing careers, even though the men studied and worked alongside the female students. Before Bellevue I had no idea that somewhere in America there were men who actually wished to become nurses. That

I easily made assumptions based on ignorance was just beginning to dawn on me.

Three days after school started, we freshmen woke up to find ourselves in the news. Both the *New York Herald Tribune* and the *New York Daily News* ran stories and pictures of us in our first Nursing Arts class, looking smart and attentive and hanging onto instructor Maggie Caller's every word. Those were the first and last pictures of our class in civilian clothes.

Our civvies were soon replaced by the Bellevue student uniform, blue-and-white-striped, below-the-calf dresses, starched white collars and cuffs, white apron and bib, starched, standard regulation nurses' caps, and black shoes and stockings. For the next three years I would never look into my closet and wonder, "What do I wear today?"

Before school started, we each received *The Four Forty Handbook*. The pages between its blue-and-white-striped cover spelled out uniform traditions and the off-duty look expected of us: skirts, sweaters, and blouses, and for Sundays, dresses and tailored suits. Slacks or pedal pushers were acceptable for the beach or bowling. No mention of blue jeans which only farmers and cowboys wore until Calvin Klein made them fashionable.

Turning up on the pages of two major New York City newspapers was heady stuff for us, a bunch of lowly "probies," shorthand for on probation and the label that set us apart from the upper classes during our first six months of school. To be a probie meant, "Watch your step. You're not home free." Somebody could still decide you didn't measure up to Bellevue's standards and send you packing. I was brash enough to tell myself, "It's Bellevue on probation, not me." Of course, I kept that thought to myself because I didn't really believe it.

I knew none of the one-hundred-eighty-nine other students and didn't care to know them early on, except to imagine which of them occupied the seat that should have been my friend, Martha's. Whoever she might be, I resented her.

At home in Akron, I had shared a room with Connie. Here, each student had her own room on either side of a long corridor whose floors were polished to a military shine. Halfway down one side of the corridor, a bathroom area large enough to handle half a dozen girls at a time announced itself. Like our rooms with their single window, twin-sized metal frame bed, desk of matching metal, straight chair, and built-in closet, the bath area was utilitarian, the toilets, sinks, mirrors, and showers built for efficiency not beauty. The absence of bathtubs was one more thing for me to get used to.

As I wandered the public rooms and hallways getting a lay of the land when I first arrived and got unpacked, I had overheard some of the girls saying that we had classmates from exotic-sounding places. There was the girl from Malta, a dot on the map off the north coast of Africa. And another one from Martinique, a Caribbean island of French-speaking Black people. Between our freshman class, and the junior and senior classes, Bellevue seemed to have drawn students from every corner of the world. Even so, most of the girls came from New York State, or one of the city's five boroughs. One girl came from Stuyvesant Town, the huge middle-income apartment complex a few blocks south of Bellevue, on First Avenue.

From September until Christmas, I fantasized that I could somehow get my old life back. I hoped I could convince my mother to let me come back home. If she knew how miserable I felt being away from her and Connie, she might relent. I might even make her feel guilty that she had pushed me out of my comfortable home for a second time—and this time before I was ready. But her will proved stronger than mine. Something I suppose she had counted on. And after a while I got used to the classroom routine and actually enjoyed learning the foundation and theories of nursing practice. Those first six months—except for a couple of brief forays across the street to the hospital where we came face-to-face with the reality of a mammoth municipal hospital, ministering to mostly poor people in all the various stages of sickness—felt the way I imagined college life, albeit a college teaching only nursing-related subjects.

Trips to the mailbox room were part of our daily routine and I anxiously looked for and sometimes found a letter written in my mother's tight and orderly hand. Or better yet, one of her letters along with a package whose size and weight suggested that it might contain a couple dozen of her plain and simple tea cakes, made from a recipe handed down from her father, something she had baked as a special treat for me. A taste of home.

Within the first year I discovered a couple of sources of extra income, and they were no further than Stuyvesant Town and its neighbor Peter Cooper Village, two huge apartment complexes just blocks from the school. Hundreds of families lived in those apartments. Families with kids. Families that needed babysitters. And who better than a student nurse to look after your kids if you were a couple wanting an evening out on the town? Or a wife wanting to do some kid-free shopping? In no time I built myself a full client list. It wasn't Lord & Taylor's department store, and I didn't get to dress up for work. My friend, Mildred Bugg—Millie Bugg for short—teased me for usually choosing a babysitting job over a date. But I was happy to again be earning some money on my own and took pride in sometimes sending some of it home to my mother. My clients included a Black symphony orchestra conductor, the first I had ever met or even knew existed. I had mixed feelings about watching his kids though, because the family had two Siamese cats that lounged on the apartment windowsills eyeing me as if I were a criminal. And then there was Sybil Trent, a white woman and former radio host of "Let's Pretend."

Her show had been one of my Saturday morning favorites as a kid. Taking a break from my chores, I'd lay on my belly near the radio and let my imagination soar. I couldn't have imagined back then that one day I'd be in charge of making Sybil Trent's two boys eat their peas. Or that the youngest one would grow up to be the renowned restaurateur, Drew Nieporent.

The first six months of school we existed in the bubble of the classroom, learning anatomy and physiology, diet and nutrition, pharmacology (taught by a good-looking male instructor, Mr. Obermeyer), and microbiology which I was close to failing before I got it through my thick head that there were no tricks to the instructor's exam questions. The questions were simple, with simple answers. I had a problem taking the questions at face value; I made them more complex than the instructor intended, imagining what she *might be asking*. Fortunately, that insight hit me in time to get a handle on my over-thinking mind. I completed the course with a decent final grade and the understanding that sometimes things are just as simple as they appear. Nothing more, nothing less.

As "probies" we learned the finer points of nursing arts, the nitty-gritty of bedside nursing care that included taking vital signs, writing notes in charts, giving baths and placing and removing bedpans and urinals, and giving shots in the butt or the deltoids. These last procedures we practiced on Mrs. Chase, a full-sized dummy who endured our tentative, sometimes clumsy and rough handling with an unflappable serenity. Whereas Mrs. Chase was unable to complain or ask questions, real patients could and would once we started spending time on Bellevue's crowded wards. And that prospect scared me. I was still not ready for the real thing, but realized at the same time that there was no turning back.

To make our big class more manageable we were divided by alphabet into two groups according to our last names, A to L and M to Z. My half went first to the surgical floors, while the other group got assigned to medicine. Then both groups switched before moving on to other rotations in urology, gynecology and obstetrics, newborn nursery, chest, operating and recovery rooms, and the other services. And there were the psychiatric wards on 30th Street and First Avenue. Thirtieth Street, at least in New York, meant crazy, and gave Bellevue its infamous identification as an insane asylum.

My second year at Bellevue I saw my first hydrocephalic baby and panicked. *I can't touch it,* I thought, and quickly looked away from the bed where the baby lay. The ward instructor, the RN responsible for teaching students the finer points of in-service care, was explaining what we were expected to learn in our rotation through the hospital's pediatric wards. I tried to listen but the sharp fear rising inside me blocked out most of her words.

Down past the metal railings of the baby's bed rested a head, huge and flat and almost as wide as the mattress. Small dark eyes held me in their gaze. I turned away. *If she assigns me to care for one of these babies, I'll leave school. I won't be able to do it.*

A few more words about the patients and our duties before the instructor crossed her arms over her starched chest and glanced at each of us as if memorizing our faces. She then began giving us our assignments. My body stiffened and I took a step back. *I just won't be able to do it.* She called out a few names and then came to mine. "Miss Tolliver, your patient will be...," and she pointed to a bed at the far end of the ward. *Oh, thank you Lord*, I said under my breath when I reached my patient's bedside. The child looked weak, but that's all.

Defying the odds, a second day, then a third day passed before I got the assignment I had dreaded. By then, miracle of miracles, I was ready. Over the previous days, I had watched the mother of the baby whose appearance had scared me show up the same time every day and with great tenderness, gently wash her baby, turn him, and speak Spanish to him. Obviously poor like almost everyone who came to Bellevue, this mother performed the infant's daily care, and no doubt staved off the bedsores, the pneumonia, or some other ailment that, given her baby's condition, could have killed him. She gave real bedside nursing care, without the title or the training. Only her mother's love.

We worked everywhere but the prison ward, though we felt its presence. Once I even witnessed a prisoner trying to escape, zigzagging across a fenced-in space behind the hospital, where an armed corrections officer tackled and handcuffed him, as patients and staff raced to the windows to watch, and pigeons roused by the shouting and scuffling scattered, and flew from the yard to roost on nearby rooftops.

A large space between the buildings, where medical and surgical patients were housed in separate wings, saw another kind of show when the Ringling Brothers Barnum & Bailey circus came to town. We wheeled our young pediatric patients outside onto the hospital grounds and the building's large balconies, in their hospital beds or wheelchairs, trailing their IV tubes with us students carefully guiding the metal poles from which hung bottles of saline or dextrose. The children watched wide-eyed as an elephant or two, and their trainers, led a parade of exotic animals into the yard, and red-nosed clowns clomped along in oversized shoes, stumbling and faking falls, anything to get a laugh. I laughed right along with the kids, marveled that the acrobats looked a lot older up close, and learned that not all medicine comes in a pill or injection.

Of all our rotations my favorite was easily the newborn nursery. I adored the smell of those little beings, their breath sometimes sweet, sometimes sour. And their bodies sometimes even stinky. I loved the curl of their tiny hands around my finger or thumb. Come feeding time, we bundled the babies up and tucked them into rolling carts, half a dozen babies, each in his or her own compartment. Precious cargo that we treated almost like cartons of eggs that we pushed onto the maternity ward and deposited with their mothers, most of whom chose to bottle feed their babies. For reasons I never figured out, many of the Puerto Rican mothers at that time favored the name Nelson for their newborn boys. And no matter how dark their complexions, the Puerto Rican babies were always checked off as white on their birth certificates.

As a student, and later as a graduate nurse, I found my comfort zone in the operating room. It suited my inclination to go for instant gratification. Most patients came into the OR with a bad appendix, broken arm, diseased intestine, troublesome gallbladder—something that needed fixing— and after anesthesia and surgery, they left in better shape. Or, in the case of Cesarean sections, women left with a new baby. Though I had little to no experience with cars—my family didn't have one and I flunked high school driver's training—I came to think of the OR like an auto body shop. The surgeon was the chief mechanic, the nurses, interns, and medical students his assistants. The chief mechanics, all specialists in their body part, from eyes to bones to nerves and internal organs, had often achieved celebrity status and everyone in the OR from nurse's aides to the head nurse deferred to them. "Dr. So-and-So is operating tomorrow, make sure you have such-and-such instruments—or his favorite retractor—or the clamp named after him," the head nurse cautioned.

Scrubbed and gowned, waiting for the great man's arrival—I never saw or scrubbed with a female surgeon—I took my place standing on a step stool, within easy reach of a tray of instruments beside the sterile field of the patient's torso, beneath a massive overhead light and, with a small audience watching from the windowed balcony, I braced myself. When the surgeon—also scrubbed, gowned, and gloved—stepped in between me and the anesthesiologist, mumbled something behind his mask and held out an open hand I made sure he got the right clamp, or chisel and hammer if he was an orthopedic guy. And the performance was on.

Occasionally things went off script when a medical student grew queasy and fainted, hopefully falling backward onto the floor and never headfirst into the sterile field of instruments, sponges, and draped, opened-up parts of the human body being operated on.

At the end of a day in the OR, important things had been accomplished and I had been part of it. I had played a role in making life better for someone. I would probably never see that someone again, or carry them home with me in my mind, or worry about them. I felt comfortable with that balance of being involved, yet also detached.

As I got to know many of my classmates, I made best friends with Sylvia Rivers from St. Albans, a middle-class enclave in the borough of Queens. Sylvia was four years older than me, and in my eyes epitomized the sophisticated and smart New York woman. She had graduated from Hunter College, which earned her a place on the fast track of study at Bellevue, allowing her to finish her training six months ahead of the rest of us with a bachelor's degree in nursing instead of the diploma awarded the three-year students. Sylvia played bid whist. In college, she had pledged Delta (America's oldest and most prestigious Black sorority), and she knew about art and about books that I had not read or even heard of.

Sylvia and some of my other new friends occasionally invited me to spend weekends at their homes. On these visits I saw that not every family behaved like mine. For instance, Sylvia's mother constantly scolded her about one thing or another. "Sister, you didn't put the top back on that jar right," she would say, her face in a perpetual frown. She rarely spoke a loving word to her daughter, never called her "honey," or "sweetie." No matter how accomplished Sylvia seemed to my eyes, to her mother she was never enough. Sylvia's stepfather, Mr. Johnson, a dark chocolate-colored, easy-going man, seemed to have few worries. He and I shared a love of his wife's extraordinary buttermilk biscuits, and "Biscuit" became his nickname for me.

Another good friend, Jersey girl Millie Bugg, and her family, often took me along on their day trips to the beach or Lake Sebago, a favorite of theirs in New York State. Between Millie, her three sisters, her mother, Mae, and father, Otis, the Bugg family covered the spectrum of colors possible among colored folks—something not uncommon in Black families—from sister Bab's "high yella," to sister Doris' shade darker, to Millie's caramel, to Joanie's medium chocolate, to Mother Mae's deep brown. Mr. Bugg, and Sylvia's stepfather, Mr. Johnson, gave me, a girl who grew up without a man around the house, a chance to see how girls with fathers in their lives might have perspectives on life different from mine. In their homes the men were boss, or at least their wives made them think so. In mine, my mother was boss. My mother made and managed the money. She doled out the punishment and she decided when her daughters deserved treats. My mother baked the cakes, changed the furnace filters, and laid the new linoleum tiles when our hallway began to look shabby. The experience taught me that living with only one parent didn't rob me of anything, as some people claimed, if that one parent was loving and capable.

Jewish people were a foreign breed to me growing up in Akron, and I never knew any before Bellevue and Linda Seeman. A petite, dark-haired girl, with an easily stereotyped New York accent, Linda lived at the end of the hall on our dorm floor and when she went home it was to the Bronx. As her guest, I got acquainted with her parents, with certain Jewish traditions, and with lox and bagels. In New York City, and at Bellevue with my new friends, I took note of other cultures and customs. Back home the difference between people had always come down to the simplest of distinctions: people were Black or white (whites were honkies in our neighborhood lingo), and Catholic or everything else.

A rarity in my nursing school days was to see a Black man show up among the white male medical students who passed through. When one of these creatures appeared in my senior year, I made no secret that I was eager to meet him. Mostly I just locked eyes with him whenever his group made rounds with the interns, residents, and attending doctors on a ward where I was assigned. He got the message and before long he introduced himself. A few more flirtatious encounters on the ward on my part, and he invited me to the movies. We saw *Singin' in the Rain*. I was thrilled, sitting beside him in the dark and imagining my own movie of the two of us becoming a couple, going off into the sunset together. He was sweet and polite, linking my arm in his as he walked me back to the nurses' residence. We parted outside the building with him giving me a soft peck on the cheek. "Thanks for the lovely evening," he said. "We'll do it again, soon." He next invited me not to a movie but to his room at the hospital.

I had never been to that part of Bellevue and didn't know quite what to expect. I knocked on the door and when he answered my jaw dropped. There he stood, backlit by a lamp from inside his room and naked as a jaybird. No shorts. No shirt. No pants. Nothing. I sucked in all the air my lungs could hold before my glance dropped to the space between his thighs. "What's the matter?" he asked. "You never seen a Black dick?"

Back at the residence I rushed to my friend Millie Bugg's room to replay the scene for her. "Can you believe it? He was butt naked. Butt naked," I said, emphasizing each word and answering my own question before allowing Millie to weigh in. "I couldn't believe it." Her eyes wide, she leaned in to make sure she had heard me right, "He really asked if you had ever seen a Black dick?" I nodded and she continued, "And what did you say?" I told her I was too shocked to say anything. I just backed away from the door to his room and made a beeline for the residence. She was the first person I'd had a chance to tell about the encounter.

If I had had the presence of mind, or the courage, I could have stood my ground outside his room and told him that in my training so far I had seen all kinds of dicks: small ones, big ones, short, long, white, brown, yellow and yes, even some Black ones when I gave bed baths to male patients, or helped them use bedpans and urinals, or checked their catheters when emptying their urinal bags, or even inserting rubber tubing into male urethras during catheterization procedures. During my OR rotation I had even seen a penis riddled with cancer, just before it was amputated. But none of those dicks had been in a state of erection, like his. True I had never seen such a sight before (except for my fat and crazy cousin Donald). More to the point I hadn't been prepared for the owner of this one to use his Black dick to bully or boast. Millie and I would laugh about the Black-dick doctor for years afterwards, noting that he never asked me out again, marveling that at the time of the incident she and I were nineteen or twenty years old—and still virgins.

The journey from probie to graduate nurse had its ceremonial rites of passage. The most auspicious and public of these occasions—the capping ceremony—mixed solemnity, satisfaction, and joy at having reached a most important milestone: we had survived our first twelve months. On that evening, with the auditorium darkened at one point, lit only by the candlelight from the old-fashioned candleholders each student held, it was official. Family and friends looked on as each girl replaced her freshman's standard-issue nurse's cap with the organdy cupcake. The Bellevue cap. The men of our class received the Mills School insignia to wear on their uniforms. One year down, two to go.

Our next high point came the following year when we exchanged our black shoes and stockings for white ones. And finally, our graduation day, June 11th, 1959, when we donned smart looking long-sleeved white uniforms for the New York University graduation and stood as a class when our school was called. But since we still had three more months of school, graduation day was more for ceremony for our families and friends than it was the real end of our Bellevue days.

My mother came in from Ohio, and with my Aunt Clarice, happily witnessed a day both women had envisioned for the last three years. For Clarice, the occasion settled an old score against Bellevue's now-outdated admissions policy. For my mother, it validated her choice of a nursing career for me. And for me, it meant I'd stuck things out for thirty-six months, despite my early resistance and lingering doubts, surprising myself and not disappointing people who believed in me and had my best interests at heart. Millie Bugg remembered graduation day as "hotter than hell." So hot, that my mother—accustomed to stomping the pedals of a pressing machine in the heat of a dry cleaners—took off her shoes, and hiked part of the way to the graduation ceremony in stocking feet. "Honey, these old dogs are worn out. And high heels don't help."

10—Not The Right Stuff
Time to move on

After graduation when I started collecting my first paychecks, I talked Sylvia into going along with me on a new venture and we signed up for classes at the Ophelia DeVore School of Charm. I was thrilled when she agreed. Besides the tuition receipts making our enrollment official, the school bestowed on us a grey, fake leather hatbox with a strap for hanging the thing over your wrist. The hatbox held our makeup, assorted beauty supplies, and the required high-heeled black pumps for when we practiced prancing down the runway.

DeVore's charm school included classes in fencing, applying make-up, sitting, and standing with good posture, all things that were supposed to help us make the best impressions if and when the rare chance of being considered for a modeling assignment came along.

If you were one of the lucky people—one of the chosen— you graduated from the charm school and joined the roster of the other part of Miss DeVore's business: the Grace Del Marco Modeling Agency. While Ophelia DeVore existed in real life, I couldn't say the same for Grace Del Marco, but the name gave the agency a certain aura of glamour.

Miss DeVore had the Black modeling agency market all
to herself back then, and a white agency like Eileen Ford
could have cared less. The phrase itself—Black model—was
practically an oxymoron. Still, every so often an ad agency or
a clothing designer hired one of DeVore's clients: the dark
skinned and elegant Helen Williams, or the equally elegant
but fair skinned LaJeune Hundley, curvy Cecelia Cooper—a
first Black Miss Cannes Film Festival—the slim Beverley
Valdez, and the statuesque and dimpled Audrey Smaltz with
her bigger-than-life personality. On the male side, the tall,
suave, and handsome Hal DeWindt and Albert Popwell.
Other Del Marco clients like Emily Yancey and Diahann
Carroll had stage and screen ambitions that Miss DeVore
helped hone.

Through the agency I picked up a few modeling jobs,
never a means of putting food on the table, but enough to
feed my dreams of one day putting nursing permanently
behind me. That time was not then. And not in modeling.
Plus, I had made the financially foolish decision to move out
of the nurses' residence, where rent was twenty dollar a
month and ninety cents bought three meals a day, and into
my own apartment, paying ninety dollars a month, food not
included. Paying rent on my own was out of the question. I
needed a roommate. Again, I turned to Sylvia, and she
shared expenses on a tiny studio in the nineties on Second
Avenue in Manhattan, a place so small it could fit only a
couple of twin beds, disguised during the day as couches
covered in blue-striped spreads. We hung a few art prints on
the wall and that was it for decorating.

Both Sylvia and I worked at Bellevue, less than half an
hour's bus ride downtown from our apartment. I worked
days in the OR and checked in with the Del Marco agency on

my days off. Mostly it was for nothing. Someone like me—
too short and not shaped for runway work—never made it to
first base on fashion calls. And I rarely got past the opening-
round interview with commercial photographers or
advertisers looking to book a young Black woman to sell
their soap or cigarettes.

Sylvia's mother and brother constantly badgered her
about being a single woman living in New York. "It just
looks so bad," her mother insisted. Sylvia eventually gave in
and moved back home to St. Albans. Desperate to find
someone to take on Sylvia's half of the rent, I turned to
another classmate, Teddi Ufirer, who saved the day. An
intense Jewish girl whose father had been with the city's
health department, Teddi was dating a doctor named
Seymour and I figured if Teddi had her way, she and
Seymour would be married before long, and the roommate
search would be on again. I was right about the wedding, but
before that happened a mysterious incident scared me into
giving up the apartment altogether. Returning home alone
one evening, I climbed the stairs and as I approached my
door, I spotted my portable record player sitting outside the
door, a door that had been locked and showed no signs of
forced entry. I slept in fits and starts that night, startled
awake by the slightest noise that might be the burglar
returning to finish his job. First thing the next morning I
called my Aunt Clarice and she agreed to let me move back
into the Dunbar with her. I never got to the bottom of the
record player mystery. But I took the incident as a sign that
it was time for me to move on, literally. Fortunately, a friend
of my friend Millie Bugg was in the market for a studio
apartment, and he took over my lease.

As chance would have it, my aunt's friend, Miss Wiggins, passed away while I was with Clarice, and Clarice talked the Dunbar management into letting me take over the now-vacant one-bedroom apartment. The rent was thirty-two dollars a month, including utilities, something even I could afford.

After a year and a half at Bellevue, I left to work nights in the OR at Flower-Fifth Avenue, a much smaller hospital and not as far downtown. I had in mind that I could work nights, look for the other kinds of work during the day, and when things were slow and I was sleepy, I could catch a quick nap on one of the operating room tables.

I had started to look outside of nursing for my life's work not long after graduating from Bellevue. From the start I knew I would. The turning point came one evening in the Bellevue Emergency Ward where I was working as a per diem nurse—meaning I was a day worker, not on staff. A young man and his sister were rushed in, and the ER team began working on them. Vital Signs. IV's. Oxygen. EKG machines and other monitors. The works. The patients had been hurt in an automobile accident. An older brother, only slightly injured, had been behind the wheel of their car.

Within what seemed minutes, the two young people were pronounced dead of their internal injuries. Their deaths haunted me for days afterward. The tragedy of two young people dying despite the efforts of one of the best emergency teams at the best trauma center in New York, or the country for that matter, left me with more questions than answers about life and death and the razor thin boundary between the two.

I imagined their older brother, the survivor, and how he would live the rest of his life with the experience of his siblings' deaths. I wondered why the accident that left the older brother with barely a scratch had sent his brother and sister to their early graves. What roles had chance and choice played in the outcome? Had the older brother been speeding? Could he have saved his siblings by slowing down? Taking a different route? Was another driver at fault? I kept picturing the emergency room filled with doctors and nurses, and emergency equipment and people rushing around, opening up sterilized trays, taking vital signs—and none of it was enough.

It was the memory of that day playing like a record stuck on replay in my head that made me want to quit, to give up. I needed to make my life's work something else. I was not strong enough, didn't have the right stuff to be a nurse, at least not the kind of nurse I had in mind.

11—Right in the Wrong Place

Taking Chances

In 1963, New York's preparation to host the World's Fair was in full swing. And when I got a call to be interviewed for a photo shoot on the fairgrounds in Queens, I was on cloud nine. I not only got the modeling job, but the photographer said he needed a man to pose with me as we were supposed to be a couple visiting the Fair. Did I know anyone? I thought right away of Dallas Selsey, a friend and neighbor in the Dunbar apartments. Dallas and his wife Karen had just a few months earlier played matchmaker, introducing me to Charles Attale, a New York City fireman and a close friend. When I met Charles—whom everyone called "Pop"—for the first time no bells and whistles went off. No fireworks. And in a way I thought that was a good sign. By then I'd had enough of heady romantic infatuations. Pop seemed easygoing and a little exotic, a life-long Brooklynite with more than a touch of the Caribbean and a taste for the good life. We started dating.

The photo shoot with Dallas went off without a hitch. It was November 22nd, a brisk, sunny day. When the photo session ended, Dallas took off for his office. I decided to take the subway from Queens into Manhattan. Somewhere between the two boroughs I heard the news: President Kennedy had been shot in Dallas. I came out of the subway and started walking along Fifth Avenue, past store windows, my eyes not registering what was in those windows. I passed people clustered at street crossings. Cars and buses rolled by. It was New York like it always was. Yet everything was changed. I continued walking for blocks, saw people crying and holding other people. Saw people watching TV sets in store windows. Saw a middle-aged white man in a business suit walking toward me and as he passed by, he spoke the only words I recall from that walk down Fifth Avenue, words heavy with hatred. "He got what he deserved."

Over the next days at my Aunt Clarice's the two of us spent hours sitting on the sofa in front of her TV, eating our meals off of TV trays.

Images on the TV screen displaced all my thoughts about careers, photo shoots, dating, finding a new apartment. Kennedy in an open car, waving to the crowds in Dallas. Kennedy slumped in his seat. Jackie Kennedy turned from the President and reaching over the car's trunk. Lyndon Johnson taking the presidential oath of office. Jack Ruby. Lee Harvey Oswald holding his abdomen. Law officials, their faces frozen in astonishment. Jackie Kennedy veiled in black holding the hands of her two small children. The boy, saluting as his father's horse-drawn coffin rolled past.

In early 1964, still holding down my night job as an OR scrub nurse, I landed a day job with the World's Fair in the Hollywood Pavilion cast as one of Cleopatra's handmaidens. The Hollywood Pavilion, one in a collection of purportedly authentic movie sets hauled in from Hollywood and wherever, included a set from Cleopatra, the movie infamously starring Liz Taylor and Richard Burton whose performances on-screen, and sizzling off-camera romance, generated weekly tabloid headlines. For all anyone of us being paid to populate the Hollywood Pavilion knew, Taylor and Burton may have never even set foot on that piece of real-estate.

The half a dozen of us handmaidens included Yvonne, a petite bronze beauty from Jamaica with a blindingly brilliant smile and a Caribbean-inflected English accent. She and I were the only dark-skinned maidens. But you'd never have known that if you saw only the handmaidens' legs. All of our legs, including those of the white girls, were the same shade of dirty tan. Apparently when the management responded to our complaint about the chilly spring weather, someone had the bright idea to have us wear tights and they never bothered to check the color. The tights did nothing to enhance our costumes, white satin-y, short, sleeveless, low-cut tunics over which we piled on our sweaters and coats whenever we were off-stage, which was quite a bit because our handmaiden role was simple: trail Cleopatra onstage every hour, waving tall ostrich-plumed fans, and arrange ourselves around her once she seated herself—after a dramatic flourish of course—on her throne. And we were to smile if any tourists showed up with cameras. It was easy money.

Other sets from well-known movies—a couple of them Westerns—made up the Hollywood Pavilion. But sets without much action lacked the magic of Hollywood as the management soon realized. So, they called in a choreographer to spice things up and a dancers' audition was scheduled at a studio in Manhattan. Nearly everyone from the Hollywood Pavilion showed up because Tex the stage manager, along with his wife, had warned us either we dance, or our days on the Hollywood Pavilion were numbered. The audition was fun and the dancing mostly freestyle. I gave it my all and ended up making the cut. A few days later, back in Queens, the director/choreographer called a rehearsal, this time with a real dance routine. No more freestyle. And some of the dancers who showed up were not from the Hollywood Pavilion, they were real dancers who had appeared in real Broadway shows. They spoke the language of dance. They knew when to step right, when to go left, when to kick, and when to twirl.

"Are you sure you're in the right place?" the director/choreographer asked me after calling me aside during the first break in the rehearsal. "Yes," I said. "I'm sure."

Back at the Cleopatra set, Tex, the Pavilion manager, informed me that I had a choice: return to my handmaiden's job, or keep showing up with the dancers every day and be fired in two weeks. "You'll have the handmaiden's job as long as I'm here," Tex assured me. "I'll think about it," I told him, not sure myself what there was to think about.

The next day I told Tex that I was choosing to stay with the dancers. Overnight I did some simple arithmetic and figured out that two weeks as a dancer at double my wages as a handmaiden was better than continuing to fan Cleopatra with no certainty of how long that job would last. Tex gave me a "you've gotta be kidding" look. A week later I learned that both Tex and his wife had been pink slipped. So much for his guarantee of my handmaiden spot.

The money I earned from the World's Fair went into a kitty for my wedding. Since the summer Charles and I had been dating, and he also got a job at the Fair as a security guard. I said yes when he asked me to marry him and we set a date for August 29th, my mother's birthday.

News of my engagement and wedding did not thrill my mother. First of all, she wished I'd have the wedding in Akron with all of our relatives and friends there. She had met Charles just once, when we came to Ohio for Christmas. By then we were engaged, and I showed her my ring. She couldn't understand that either. Blue pearl? Why not a diamond like most engagement rings? As a Christmas present Charles bought me a guitar. I think he found it in a pawn shop. It was what I had asked for. Another of those things I thought I would learn to do...someday.

I had started meeting with Father Bill Houston, a Black priest at St. Peter Claver Church in Brooklyn for my instruction as a non-Catholic, as word got around to my Ohio relatives that I was getting married. "Why is Melba not getting married in Akron? Why to a Catholic?" And most puzzling to them: "Why is she marrying a foreigner?" my Uncle Al asked, speaking not just for himself, but for my mother's entire family. My family never knew any West Indians, probably never even heard of them. And it made no difference to them that Pop and his four sisters were all born in America.

At the other extreme was Pop's mother, Evelyn. She also was not thrilled about the marriage. She wanted a West Indian daughter-in-law, preferably one from Trinidad. Evelyn had big dreams for her son and youngest child. He was to become a lawyer. In the front hall of her home on Lincoln Road stood a tall, very old oak bookcase with glass door panels. Evelyn bought it for the purpose of one day housing Charles's law books.

Despite her many years in the States, Mrs. Attale still spoke with a heavy accent, maintained many of the Island's traditions, customs, and cuisine. She took over preparations for the wedding cake months ahead of the date. It was to be a black fruitcake, a Trinidadian specialty that called for a long marinating of the fruit in lots of rum. The wedding would be at St. Peter Claver Roman Catholic Church and reception in the Crown Heights brownstone of Charles' sister June. June had married well, to a doctor. But he had left her and taken his prestige with him. Nearly two years after she opened her home for our wedding reception, June overdosed. The word suicide was never used when the Attales talked about June's dying.

The day of the wedding, the organ music rose, filling the church with the familiar chords announcing the bride. On cue all heads turned toward me as I started down the aisle looking straight ahead, aware that in some of the pews people were probably thinking, *What kind of bride walks down the aisle alone? It's a shame. You'd think one of her male relatives would have escorted her.* To walk unescorted down the aisle after my closest uncle said he couldn't come to the wedding, probably looked to some like yet another of my odd choices.

The bridal party stood in a tight half circle, waiting. I kept my attention on the bridesmaids in their powder blue gowns, the groom and groomsmen in grey morning coats, Father Bill Houston in his clerical garb. And behind my veil I struggled with my own thoughts: *Why am I doing this? I don't want to be married. Too late now.*

A quick glance to my left and I saw my mother and my aunts Clarice and Rovena. Each wore a pleasant expression, a hat, white gloves, and a proper, related-to-the bride, pastel dress. These Baptist-raised sisters, Georgia-born Midwesterners, had never set foot in a Catholic church before.

I had chosen the date for my wedding, my mother's birthday, to honor her. But things were not turning out the way I had imagined. I had messed up all around. I'd let the Attales take charge of most of the wedding details, reducing my mother's role to that of being mostly a guest at her own daughter's wedding. I had seemed inconsiderate of my Ohio relatives. And now I was about to say, "I do," to pledge to honor and obey a man I cared for but could not honestly say I wanted to be married to until one of us died. Compared to friends who married at eighteen or twenty, I was considered an older bride. But the way I looked at things I was young enough to have many years ahead to be a wife. The reality of it made me worry.

Six months later, the Selseys, Charles, and I waited at JFK airport for a flight to Port of Spain, Trinidad, on a delayed honeymoon for us and a chance to be revelers in Trinidad's spectacular Carnival, when we heard the news: assassins had shot and killed Malcom X. Once again, "the chickens had come home to roost."

On the honeymoon, a time when newlyweds were expected to still be aglow over the big event, Charles and I had our first big argument over who was to blame for the Selseys leaving earlier than they had planned, Charles's charge that I was standoffish with his relatives, and mine that he tried to boss me around. Our angry words penetrated the bedroom walls and made our hosts—Charles's Aunt Sybil and her husband, Jackie—decide it was time for a walk on the beach—separately—to cool off.

Things got off to a bad start the first morning when I spotted a bicycle in the yard and decided to take a spin on it before breakfast. I rode about a mile before turning around to retrace my ride. In my path stood a muscular brown dog, breathing heavily, his teeth bared. With trembling hands, I gripped both ends of the handlebars, slid off the seat, trying to keep my moves slow and controlled, and eased the bike's front wheel between the dog and me. I looked around in the hope that somebody, maybe the owner, would suddenly appear. No such luck. The dog squeezed out a low, rumbling growl, and took a stutter step toward me. I started running and jumped on the bike, my feet finding the pedals, my legs and heart pumping. The dog's teeth caught me just above my ankle, then let go. I kept pedaling, ignoring a sharp pain where blood was staining my pants.

Later that day, after my wound had been tended to, I hobbled off with Charles to a small park in Port of Spain, where a group of seventy or so World War Two veterans awaited the appearance of Queen Elizabeth. Charles's Aunt Sybil had used her government position with Trinidad's equivalent to the U.S. Veteran's Administration to add our names to the guest list, assigned to spots well behind the veterans. My injured leg made standing at attention in high heels uncomfortable, and I worried if the dog that bit me might be rabid. But I was excited about the chance to witness a historic event, a queen's first visit to her former colony. The veterans, dressed for the occasion in suits or pants and unmatched jackets, stood three rows deep and spoke quietly among themselves. They seemed oblivious to the heat except for the occasional man who plucked a handkerchief from his breast pocket, wiped his sweaty forehead, and wedged the hanky back into place. On every chest, a ribbon or a medal, some sign that these old men belonged to a closed and dwindling fraternity.

Also waiting just outside the park, uniformed school children holding small Union Jacks and Trinidadian flags, fidgeted, and peered down the street. They were first to spot the caravan of black Rolls-Royces, and to greet it with a burst of cheers and applause, shouts, and flag-waving, as it pulled up to the park gate. The old men drew themselves up to attention as the royal entourage approached. What I took to be the Queen's ladies-in-waiting passed, then Prince Philip, whose suit called forth the image of an aged tailor bent over a workbench hand-stitching it. And finally, the Queen. Like an ocean wave, the men bowed as she passed. I started to bow but stopped. This might be my only chance to see a real queen up close and I wanted to get a good look.

Her dress, blue, short-sleeved, and without a wrinkle, revealed her forearms with their dusting of soft hair. She wore immaculate white gloves, and the handles of her handbag hung over her wrist now held close to her chest. Her pale complexion contrasted sharply with the dark skin of her former subjects. Nodding in slow motion as she moved along the lines of ex-warriors, she smiled. And there on one front tooth was a smudge of scarlet lipstick. That broke the spell for me. Reassured me. Nobody's perfect. Not even a queen. With ladies to wait on her, she can still miss something.

Gold bangle-style bracelets—some plain, others elaborately engraved and worn in pairs—is a West Indian tradition. Charles's mother wore them, and his sisters and niece did too. Maybe to soothe hurt feelings, and maybe as something to show off to our friends back home, Charles suggested we go shopping for a pair of bangles of my own, as long as we were in the place where the tradition had so much meaning.

In the quiet of a lovely downtown jewelry store, a golden-skinned clerk with jet-black hair and who looked to be East Indian made her way over to us. "May I help you?" she asked in the lilting cadence that my ears were slowly becoming used to. As Charles and I pointed to the different bracelets, offering opinions about first one pair and then another, I replied, "We're just looking. We're interested in the bracelets." I looked up to see the clerk smiling. "Oh, you're American," she said. I turned to look behind me to see who was she speaking to, before I realized she meant me. Two thousand, two hundred and ten miles from home, in a foreign land, I was, for the first time in my experience, an American, plain and simple. An American. Without the hyphen.

12—1963
An Angry Woman

Before the day's lessons at Allen Elementary School and then at South High got started, one thing you could count on, you placed your right hand over your heart and recited these words:

> I pledge allegiance to the flag of the United States of America and to the Republic for which it stands, one nation (under God, *added on Flag Day, 1945),* indivisible with liberty and justice for all.

I rarely gave those words any thought. The pledge was just part of the school day like recess and lunchtime, geometry and pep rallies. The flag, hanging limply off to one side of the classroom and to which I was pledging my allegiance was real enough, but the United States of America? That place existed in the words and pictures in my history books, in the stories about Pilgrims and Indians sharing their first Thanksgiving, George Washington in his white wig and tri-cornered hat, Betsy Ross stitching up the American flag, cowboys taming the West, the Liberty Bell rung until it cracked and multitudes of disconnected facts to be memorized for the next test, then forgotten or deposited in the depths of my memory bank.

My United States of America existed outside the history books. And my allegiance to it was deep, informal, and written nowhere. I acted on my allegiance in my home with my mother and my sister, with other family and friends, in my neighborhood with the ordinary, everyday people like me. I never felt the need to declare myself American. I was just me, known in my immediate world as, "Sue's daughter, Connie's sister, Al and Rovena's niece, Martha's and Mary Alice's friend."

I've read and heard it said that everything changed in the 1960's. That this mythologized decade really began in earnest in 1963, the year I turned twenty-five and showing signs that I was on a mission to find my place in a country, in a culture where I didn't seem to fit. A woman. Not married. No children. A nurse not because I felt a calling but because that's what some of the people I loved and respected wanted for me while I longed for a career that I couldn't yet define or describe. A Black citizen of a nation lurching toward a war in Southeast Asia while fully engaged in one at home where the push for civil rights was met with beatings, bullets, and bombs. It was a year of violent racist rhetoric competing with strains of "We Shall Overcome."

A year for people to debate whether I and people like me were American or not and what rights I was or was not entitled to.

Halfway through 1963 I discovered that I had a voice. I found out that voice, while not easily defined, is not to be confused with sound only. That discovery coincided with me thinking seriously, deliberately, and out loud for the first time about being American.

One morning, as I rode the commuter bus from midtown Manhattan to my secretarial job in New Jersey, I read that the *New York Herald Tribune* was planning to run a series titled "Ten Negroes." (April 30th to May 12th, 1963.) Intrigued, I read on. In advertising the multi-part series of interviews, the newspaper had promised, "A powerful and provocative portrait of today's Negroes," to be reported and written by its national correspondent, the white journalist, Robert S. Bird.

I couldn't wait to read it.

Days passed and the first installment appeared, an interview with Elijah Muhammad, leader of the Black Muslims. Beneath his picture, the text said, "His Black Muslim propaganda, without question, is forcing all civil rights organizations and even Negro politicians to take another step toward harder, more extreme positions."

Next, Dr. James M. Nabrit Jr., president of Howard University. In the opening paragraph about him, the reporter posed what he called, "a bitter question that rattles in the minds of most white people in the nation's Capital." And that question? "Why don't the Negroes themselves do more to clean up crime among their own people?"

Third in the series, thirty-four-year-old Martin Luther King Jr., whom the reporter interviewed for two hours just before King traveled to Birmingham, the epicenter of racial equality protests, and where King would be jailed for the thirteenth time. Bird again posed a question he had put to others in his series. A question that he said was on the minds of most white people: "What is it that Negroes want?" King responded, saying:

Three simple words can describe the nature of the social revolution that is taking place and what Negroes really want. They are the words 'all,' 'now,' and 'here'... The mood of Negroes now is that we are Americans, and America is our home...."

After those initial interviews with high-profile figures, Bird got around to talking with a few lesser-known folks, including a twenty-seven-year-old secretary who had lived and worked for two years in Israel. "I don't know how to explain it," she told Bird, "but when I went away I completely forgot that I was a Negro, more or less." The Harlem resident said that away from the place she called home she was "treated as something special."

And then there was Vernon S. Gill, a senior student at Howard University. Bird was "flabbergasted" when Gill wouldn't discount the possibility of being president of the United States one day. "I wouldn't exclude that. Seriously, I wouldn't," said Gill, whose "bold ideas" were obviously foreign territory for Bird.

I found the series a big disappointment long before Bird talked to those last few people. I had expected to learn something new about the day-to-day experiences of fed-up and angry ordinary Black people. Where were their voices in answer to those white people's questions? My frustration with the series grew. So much so that one night after work I stayed at my desk after everyone had left for the day and typed a letter to Robert S. Bird. I told him that I thought he had failed to understand what everyday life was like for Black people in America. The pent-up frustration and resentment over being ignored and made to feel invisible exploded all over Bird in my letter. This was part of my voice. Not its entirety, but a large part of it.

I never expected Bird would actually read my letter. Or respond to it. As Bird noted in the conclusion to his series, my letter was just one in an avalanche of mail from readers, Black and white, who mostly praised his reporting. Mine was not one of those. But soon after he got my letter, Bird called and very politely asked to interview me over the phone. He also asked if he could send a photographer to my home to take my picture. I said OK and a few days later the paper published my letter and my picture under the headline, "An Angry Woman."

I was surprised and pleased that my words had done more than I intended. Especially when Bird himself wrote:

> One of the bitterest, angriest, and most contemptuous letters—and one of the most literate—came from a woman. I believe her letter makes a good point and one missing from the series, and that it is a fine example of a Negro person communicating fully to the white side. So, I reproduce it in full here.

I didn't make a copy of my 1963 letter to Bird. But in 1999, while serving as the Howard R. Marsh visiting professor of journalism at the University of Michigan, I learned that the "Ten Negroes" series had been reprinted, and I was able to get a copy. Over the years I read and re-read the entire series with special attention to my letter.

I didn't see this when I wrote to Bird. But there it was on paper, in black-and-white newsprint, the words, the syntax, the sentiment, the structure—all of it—defiantly rebuking

Robert S. Bird and introducing me—an ordinary, everyday Black woman—to *Tribune* readers.

Miss Melba Tolliver, who wrote the letter.

At that late date, I also realized that the most stunning revelation of the entire series was in Bird's conclusion where he confessed to holding an ingrained preconception about Black people. He said it was a fundamental bias and that it only became obvious to him in the course of his reporting. That insight was an epiphany, a moment of self-discovery. Bird had been shown—with startling clarity—his own blind spot as a white man, as an American, and as a journalist; he saw himself as a man who believed that while Negroes might be Americans, they were a separate group of Americans. As Bird reported:

> Though I had spent much time in the last eight years on assignments involving desegregation conflicts and had watched with sympathy the Negro struggle for civil rights and equality in riot-torn places in the Deep South and here in New York City, I learned that my own "hearing" of the Negro was being obstructed.
>
> Take one seemingly simple but subtle point—their status as American citizens.
>
> I had never doubted that the Negroes were in theory full American citizens in every respect and legally entitled to all their civil rights. I knew full well that they were being systematically impeded by white groups and institutions in attaining these rights and privately I deplored that.
>
> But I felt more or less unthinkingly that they were a separate group of Americans, one which was in a slow and sure process of winning full acceptance and participation.
>
> It never occurred to me until I was deep in the interviewing of Negroes for this series that a preconception was hampering my understanding, for there is in truth only one kind of American. That is a full American, entitled to all rights, privileges, and equal enjoyment of opportunities, and all the rest, without having to earn these and without having to prove himself.

Then the sense of outrage which the Negro feels
today dawned on me. The outrage of being required,
seemingly, forever, to **earn** their way to full enjoyment
of their rights as Americans.

This was a candid and clear insight by a white journalist
admitting to his readers—in print, and in a major
newspaper—that a personal bias about Black people shaped
his thinking and therefore his reporting.

After I had become a journalist myself, I realized that
Bird had done something almost unheard of, something very
uncommon, something rare among journalists. In my
memory I could recall not one other white journalist ever
publicly coming even close to Bird's admission of personal
bias. None, admitting as Bird did, to having a blind spot in
the way they identified America's racial problem and the
treatment of Blacks by white people for whom folks like me
were invisible, or simply didn't count in *their* America.

My writing that letter to Robert S. Bird didn't turn me
into a reporter, didn't launch me as a TV anchorwoman. For
one thing in 1963 I hadn't even the most remote thoughts of
journalism as a career. But my letter did tell me something
about voice. That I had one.

From the time I could look around and see that my
American experience was nothing like the one portrayed in
the history books I read in school, I saw that people like me
were mostly missing. What I was learning didn't square with
what I saw in my neighborhood and on most of the streets
that I walked in Akron. My letter to Bird and his response to
it showed me that my words could have power. My anger
could be channeled. I was an everyday person who might

find a way to speak to some part of the America that wanted me to keep quiet.

And Bird's revelation about himself showed me that journalists have the choice to be aware of and pay attention to their own biases. They can take a chance, make the choice to be self-aware. And doing so may not only enhance the understanding of their readers and viewers, but bring the journalist to a better understanding of self, as Bird did.

Taking that a step further, journalists can also choose to question—and maybe ignore—the dictum to be "objective," understanding that all humans hold biases, and with grace we will acknowledge and work around them.

Well into my reporting experience, these insights—and the understanding that *who* tells the news matters—would largely shape my journalism practice.

I came to understand that, for the people watching me on TV or reading my words in print, I am the voice, the lens, the storyteller, the means by which my audiences can and maybe will view the people, the issues, and the places I cover as a reporter.

For the "Ten Negroes" series Bird had met with King in his small, cluttered office at the Southern Christian Leadership Conference headquarters in Atlanta. And strange as it seems, in their two hours together neither the preacher nor the journalist said a word about plans for a massive march on the nation's capital then being organized by civil rights activists.

But four months after Bird's series in which King called for sweeping executive action by President Kennedy to end discrimination in areas where jobs are tied to Federal funds, an estimated quarter of a million people flooded into the nation's capital. The March on Washington for Jobs and Freedom became the biggest demonstration of its kind in history and revealed to the nation and the world that the civil rights movement had many faces.

Mine was one of them. An everyday, ordinary, young Black American woman on my first visit to Washington, D.C., among tens of thousands of other everyday, ordinary Black people—and thousands more of different racial and ethnic backgrounds and stations in life—gathered around the reflecting pools on the National Mall demanding jobs and freedom. Most of us were people like the ones I had in mind and had attempted to speak for when I wrote to Robert S. Bird and the *Herald Tribune* criticizing the white journalist for highlighting what I called "big shots" in his "Ten Negroes" series and failing to understand what life was like for people like us in our own country.

Being part of the March on Washington on that day in 1963, I believed, was the right choice, though I had never been part of any kind of "march," or carried a picket sign. Never been attacked by vicious police dogs. Never knocked to the ground by the force of high-pressure water hoses. Never tried to buy a cup of coffee at a segregated lunch counter.

Distracted by the heat and humidity, and perhaps worried that I might get separated from my companions who had traveled by bus to D.C. in a caravan of New Yorkers organized by a local union, I gave only scant attention to the celebrities and bold-faced names who took turns at the microphones on the dais several football fields away from me.

And the part of King's speech that got my attention that day was not so much about his dream; it was about his warning. And he said,

> And those who hope that the Negro needed to blow off steam and will now be content will have a rude awakening if the nation returns to business as usual. And there will be neither rest nor tranquility in America until the Negro is granted his citizenship rights. The whirlwinds of revolt will continue to shake the foundations of our nation until the bright day of justice emerges...meeting physical force with soul force.

In January 1963, seven months before the March on Washington, George Wallace, Alabama's newly-elected governor, speaking at his inaugural, weighed in with his vision for his state and the nation: *Segregation now. Segregation tomorrow. Segregation forever.* And as the year unfolded, from Birmingham to Brooklyn, Nashville to Detroit, Memphis to Chicago, Baltimore to Boston, Savannah to Plaquemine, everyday ordinary Black people—women, men, and hundreds of children—resisted, demanding equal rights, sitting in, marching, protesting, demonstrating, organizing, picketing. In return they were fire-hosed, dog-attacked, beaten, jailed, threatened, mocked, shot, kicked, spat upon, stomped, tear-gassed, electric-prodded, bombed, and murdered.

Six months after taking office, on the second Tuesday in June, George Wallace attempted to make good on his segregationist's pledge. He staged a "standing in the schoolhouse door" confrontation with federal officials outside the University of Alabama in a symbolic act of barring the enrollment of two Black students.

Later in the evening, on the very same day, just before 8pm, I turned on the small black and white TV in my one-bedroom apartment in the Dunbar, my home in Harlem for the past year, and made myself comfortable on the bed.

In the nation's capital, President Kennedy, at the White House, was taking a seat at his desk in the Oval Office. Nearby, out of camera range, some of the President's staff waited. They included Andrew Hatcher, an assistant press secretary and the highest-ranking Black person in the Kennedy White House. In a matter of minutes, a stage manager would count the President down to begin a speech that Kennedy's advisors and inner circle were said to believe he had no choice but to make. They told him he had to use this moment to speak out against the racial violence being perpetrated against Black Americans. The president said,

> Difficulties over segregation and discrimination exist in every city, in every State of the Union, producing in many cities a rising tide of discontent that threatens the public safety. We are confronted primarily with a moral issue...whether all Americans are to be afforded equal rights and equal opportunities.

And he promised to take the next step and send Congress a strong civil rights bill.

Just before midnight, after Kennedy's speech, Medgar Evers, a thirty-seven-year-old NAACP field secretary and a US Army veteran, was in his driveway, returning home from work, when shots rang out. Evers had been shot in the back by a white supremacist. Evers died minutes later, on June 12th.

Thirty years and three trials later, Byron De La Beckwith was convicted of murdering Evers, and sentenced to life in prison.

In September, three months after Evers's murder, four black girls—Addie Mae Collins, Carole Robertson, and Cynthia Wesley, all fourteen, and Denise McNair, eleven, were killed by a bomb blast that leveled Birmingham's 16th Street Baptist Church. The girls were attending Sunday School.

In 2002, the last of the three white supremacist bombers was tried and convicted of first-degree murder.

On November 22nd, two months after the 16th Street Baptist Church was blown up, John F. Kennedy, riding in an open car in a Dallas, Texas motorcade, with his wife Jacqueline seated beside him, was shot to death.

Within hours, Lyndon Johnson took the oath of office, aboard Air Force One, succeeding the murdered Kennedy as thirty-sixth president of the United States.

Two days later, Jack Ruby, a Dallas nightclub owner, shot and killed Lee Harvey Oswald, JFK's assassin.

On November 25th, JFK's remains were interred in Arlington National Cemetery where, on June 15th, Medgar Evers had also been buried.

13—Kerner

Two societies, one black, one white, separate and unequal

When you are ignorant of the past, and unable to imagine the future, or even be fully present to everything going on around you every day, as I was in my mid-twenties, you don't know that you are in the right place at the right time. In my case that was being perfectly situated to back into the news-reporting business in the late 1960's.

"The long hot summer" is what people in the business of labeling things called the months between April and July of 1967, when urban disturbances rocked the nation, and more than three-dozen American cities erupted in arson fires and other assorted acts of rude rebellion. Two years earlier South-Central Los Angeles had undergone its own uprising, foreshadowing the worst of the riots during two weeks in July, first in Newark where twenty-three people perished, then in Detroit and Cleveland.

The rioters, mostly young Black men, fed up with white racism, frustrated with conditions that kept them trapped in ghettos not of their making, and feeling hopeless about finding jobs or otherwise cashing in on the "American Dream," tore up and burned down parts of the so-called inner cities, the urban areas where the rioters themselves lived. In predominantly Black communities, businesses burned to the ground, opportunistic looters and vandals held sway and everyday people held their breath behind locked doors and prayed for things to calm down.

Four days after Newark exploded, President Lyndon
Johnson went on television and told a national audience
that he was forming a commission to determine the "who"
and the "why" of the riots. He also asked the commission to
find out how to prevent future uprisings. In addition to Otto
Kerner, governor of Illinois, whose name came to define the
group, the eleven members of the National Advisory
Commission on Civil Disorders included John Lindsay,
Republican Liberal Mayor of New York as Vice Chairman;
two US Senators, Fred Harris, Democrat from Oklahoma
and Edward Brooke, Republican from Massachusetts; two
US Congressmen, James Corman, Democrat from California
and William McCulloch, Republican from Ohio; Roy
Wilkins, Executive Director of the NAACP; Katherine
Peden, former Kentucky Commerce Commissioner; I.W.
Abel, United Steelworkers President; Herbert Jenkins,
Atlanta Chief of Police; and Charles Thornton, Litton
Industries Chairman. The panel had no firebrand activists
from the right or the left. Its political makeup was mostly
moderate, neither progressive nor conservative. Two of the
men were Black (Wilkins and Brooke; Brook was elected in
1966 and the first Black sent to the US Senate by popular
vote since Reconstruction). Everyone else was white,
including the one female.

The Commission was thorough in its investigation. It
employed a professional staff, an advisory panel, and
consultants, as well as special and student assistants. They
held formal hearings, conducted field surveys, site visits to
riot cities, twelve-hundred-plus interviews, and had forty-
four days of intense meetings. Wrapping up their work, the
Commissioners heard every word of their nine-hundred-
page report read aloud, and debated and revised it before a

majority gave it their approval. That's according to commission member Fred Harris, the Oklahoma Senator.

On March 1st, 1968, six months after their appointment, the Commissioners presented President Johnson a wide-angled look at the rioting and identified some of the underlying causes: unemployment, poverty, substandard education, inadequate housing, police practices, jobs. Bottom line, all the usual suspects. Looking at the riots as if through a wide-angled lens and in language that pointed fingers in many directions, some of the report's most memorable observations remain in the American lexicon: "Two nations, one Black, one white, separate and unequal."

The Commission's harsh indictment of the news media came down to four words: "A failure to communicate." Not words that any business or institution that trades in observing, articulating, and explaining the world really wants to hear.

Journalist and *New York Times* columnist Tom Wicker called the Report, "a remarkable document," and he wrote in his introduction, "The single overriding cause of rioting in the cities was not any one thing.... It was all of those things and more, expressed in the insidious and pervasive white sense of the inferiority of Black men."

As news, the Kerner Report was old news. Pointing this out, Dr. Kenneth B. Clark, the distinguished scholar, sociologist, and a lead-off witness in the Kerner investigation, cited earlier riots in Chicago, Harlem, and Watts. Dr. Clark likened the investigations of those riots and the reports they inspired in 1919, 1935, 1943, and 1965 to "a kind of Alice in Wonderland—with the same picture re-shown over and over again, the same analysis, the same recommendations, and the same inaction."

And finding fault with the media was also nothing new. In 1947, the Hutchins Commission accused the media of failing to accurately portray social groups, thereby perverting judgment of minorities. And in January 1968, two months before Kerner released its findings, the Equal Employment Opportunities Commission challenged the media to hire more people of color.

Nevertheless, the Kerner Report differed substantially from previous news media critics. It lodged both its charges and its recommendations in detailed and stinging specifics. It accused the media of a "failure to communicate to their white-majority audience a sense of what life is like in Black ghettoized communities." It said that "far too often, the press acts and talks about Negroes as if Negroes do not read the newspapers or watch television, give birth, marry, die, and go to PTA meetings."

The news media companies' responses to Kerner ranged from denial, to mild, to full-blown action. And some of the doors previously shut to non-white hires began to open. As an article in the trade magazine, *Editor and Publisher*, optimistically headlined: "The Welcome Mat Is Out" for Negroes in the city rooms of American newspapers.

Even so, it wasn't as if a handful of pioneering Black journalists had not already broken barriers and forged paths before the new Black hires arrived. Ernest Dunbar at *Look* magazine, Tom Johnson, Charlayne Hunter-Gault, Earl Caldwell and Nancy Hicks at the *New York Times*, Gil Scott, and Austin Scott at the *Associated Press* were just a few of the "firsts" and "onlys."

Mal Goode, Laymond Robinson, and Bob Teague—all established newspaper men—had been hired by competing broadcast networks even before the Kerner Report. Mal had been with the *Pittsburgh Courier*, a Black-owned newspaper, and been on radio when ABC News President Jim Hagerty recruited him to come to the network and be its United Nations correspondent. Laymond Robinson, also a veteran newspaper journalist, had been one of the *New York Times's* earliest Black hires before ABC News lured him away from the old gray lady.

And Bob Teague, another *New York Times* man, had been hired by NBC News. Teague, a former football star at the University of Wisconsin, had been a highly respected sportswriter for the newspaper.

Moving from newspapers to broadcast journalism required these folks to make adjustments, working with camera crews for starters, getting the right pictures and making sure to be in synch with union rules. And no doubt they had to find a way of dealing with the white producers and technicians who resented them and didn't mind showing it.

If not for the folks who rioted, who caused "the long hot summer," there would have been no Kerner Commission. No Kerner Report. No harsh criticism of the news media. No recommendations that the news media—print and broadcast—change their newsrooms. That they recruit, train, hire, and promote Negroes to positions of responsibility in journalism. If not for the riots and the Report they prompted, the numbers of Black news professionals on daily newspapers (one percent) and in broadcasting (three percent) at the time of the 1967 riots would have surely remained predictably and pitifully few well into the future.

14—Intern

"You will never get into our union."

In 1967, major mainstream media organizations around the country, and especially in New York, were making people like me news trainees and interns (though none of them were like me and carried the scab label).

And in the spring of that year—with two years of marriage gone by and the AFTRA strike well behind me—my position with ABC News changed. No longer would I be secretary to Donald Coe, the man responsible for putting me on TV as a substitute anchorwoman. Coe informed me that ABC News was creating a news training program. He asked if I would be interested in being in it. My "Yes!" didn't surprise him. While I wasn't in on the conversations the top brass had about starting this in-house effort, I was sure the Kerner Commission's riot report played into their thinking. And offering me the chance to be their first trainee made sense. I had stepped in on short notice to fill Marlene Sanders's empty anchor chair in March, my debut had been widely publicized and received pretty good press. Plus, I was female. And Black.

With the new job came a new title: "intern." Given my nursing background, I thought I knew more than a few things about interns. A white lab coat and stethoscope went with the medical intern's job. But news intern? I soon learned that whether in a hospital or a newsroom, intern meant one thing: starting on the lowest rung of our respective career ladders. If interns in the medical field managed to tough it out, they could look forward to a residency, and after developing a specialty, they might start their own practice, be made an attending at some prestigious institution, and become so famous that a new surgical instrument, or medical discovery would bear their names.

I, on the other hand, had no clue where my internship would lead. No one had made me any promises. My current path might wind up in a dead end or lead me right back to being a secretary. In the best possible scenario, I might be offered a reporting job.

But then, a couple of months into my internship, things changed again. In late October 1967, six months after that first walkout and my TV news debut, a second nationwide strike threatened to cripple ABC and the other two broadcast networks. This time NABET, the union of engineers and technicians, walked out. And, as payback to NABET for honoring its thirteen-day strike—AFTRA called on its members, including the on-camera people, to stay away from work. Faced with this demonstration of union solidarity, ABC News executives, once again, needed to fill their empty anchor chairs, and again, they tapped me to replace Marlene Sanders on *News with the Woman's Touch*.

But now not only had my job changed, I had changed, too. Instead of seeing the exposure on national TV as a fun experience, a lark, a short break from the daily humdrum of typing, filing, and answering the phone with no ambition for a news career beyond becoming a researcher, I was a news trainee. I had high hopes for my future. I could picture myself climbing a career ladder from trainee to researcher, to one day getting hired as a full-fledged, on-air reporter.

Back in March, as a secretary, I had nothing at stake. But with the NABET strike, if I chanced being labeled a scab a second time, I feared that none of those possibilities would come to pass. Or, just as troubling, I might land an on-camera job and need to join AFTRA, only to have the union retaliate and blackball me. One of its members—a network correspondent—had already threatened as much the first day I crossed his picket line. "You'll never get into our union," he yelled as he confronted me, stared me down, red-faced and angry. The news executives now asking me to defy the NABET-led pickets were the same executives who came up with a training program offer that I chose to accept. How could I justify saying "no" to these men *now* when I had said "yes" to them just months ago? Had these people rewarded me for being a good substitute anchor, or a willing sacrificial scab? Or both?

Once I weighed my options, and despite having mixed feelings about my choice, I agreed to anchor *News with the Woman's Touch*, one more time. Part of me wanted to fill in for Marlene, but another part of me worried that the news higher-ups would cast a more critical eye on my performance this time around. I imagined them judging me differently, seeing me not as Don Coe's secretary, but as the guinea pig for their training program. This time, I felt I had a lot to lose. I let my fears undermine my self-confidence and cause me to be overly cautious. I was looking to take a big gamble on my future. A gamble I could very possibly lose. I tried hard not to even think about that.

I told myself that I had to look like I was comfortable in the anchor chair, like I knew what I was doing, even when I didn't. Despite my best efforts, I struggled with a tongue-twister on one of the newscasts. Having my gaffe reported by Robert Dallos in the pages of the *New York Times* made it especially embarrassing that I stumbled over the sentence, "Senator Stuart Symington said...." I survived the stumble and my training continued.

My first stop on the intern wheel of fortune had landed me on the network assignment desk. In that all-white, ninety-nine-percent male environment, let's just say that I stood out. Black. Female. Strikebreaker. Scab. No way would I be mistaken for one of the guys. Even the lowly desk assistant given grunt work to do was above me in the newsroom hierarchy.

Hanging around the assignment desk and Nick Archer, the man in charge of the desk and me and internship, showed me the many decisions that often go into assigning and covering a single story. I took note of the varied roles that bureau chiefs, producers, and correspondents played in shaping the day's news. These decision-makers were all white men. And, while anyone from the lowliest person taking coffee orders to the president of ABC News could suggest a story idea to the desk, the further up the hierarchy, the more likely the story idea got serious consideration. If Elmer Lower, president of ABC News, or his second-in-command, Bill Sheehan dropped by the newsroom and said he thought a certain topic should be looked into, it was.

Good news and bad marked my eighteen-month internship. The bad news: I was expected to tag along with correspondents, watch as they carried out their assignments, and volunteer to help. That was a wild hope. ABC, smallest of the big three broadcast networks, didn't have all that many correspondents, and few of them would even be found on West 66th Street on a regular basis. Those who did pass through avoided me like the plague, flatly refusing to have anything to do with me, much less allow me to shadow them.

And as for work covered by the labor/management agreements, that was out of the question unless you belonged to the Writers Guild, AFTRA, or one of the other unions representing the crafts, technicians, and camera crews. Obviously, I dared not even look like I was encroaching on any of that work. So even if anyone had been willing to have my help there was little for me to do besides simply show up every day. It was the price I paid for being a scab, the dirtiest four-letter word in the world of organized labor.

The good news: ABC had never had a news intern or a news training program. That looked to me like an opportunity, a chance to design my own training curriculum, and I took that chance when no one else seemed interested. First, I signed up for classes over the summer at New York University, trekking downtown to Greenwich Village twice a week to study Journalism 101 and news writing. ABC had agreed to foot the tuition bill. When not at NYU, and after Nick Archer thought I had learned all that was useful about how the network assignment desk fit into the scheme of things, he turned me over to the guest commentators unit. There, I mostly tried to be helpful to the producer in charge. I made and returned phone calls, guided guests to the interview area and chatted briefly with some of them. Of all the guests, the most memorable was David Halberstam, journalist and author, an authoritative figure and one of our most prominent guests who was just four years older than me. Perhaps it was his book about Robert Kennedy that had made the commentary-unit producer book him for an interview. I don't recall. But I had a copy of his book which he autographed (free books were a big perk that came with working for that unit). I thought what Halberstam wrote on an inside page of my book was pretty special, until producer Blaine Littell, white, wise and witty—and a Peabody-award winner and an author himself—pointed out to me that what Halberstam wrote for me could fit anybody.

At that point in my internship, the antagonism toward me had softened enough that after the guest commentary unit, I was assigned to perform similar chores in the special events and elections units. Even so, no way was I expecting the next turn of events in my training. And I was astonished in March 1968 to have the elections unit send me to New Hampshire for the Democratic presidential primary—my first and only out-of-town assignment as an intern. Just as surprising, I would be tagging along with Bill Lawrence, ABC News's political affairs editor. Lawrence was not only a news-department heavyweight, he was believed to be the only news analyst to predict in 1966, two years ahead of the fact, that Lyndon Johnson would not seek re-election.

By whose good graces my fortunes had changed so dramatically from the beginning of my internship to then, no one ever explained and I didn't ask. One of two really important times in my ABC tenure that I didn't ask "Why? What prompted this?" The first time had been when Don Coe put my name up to sit in for Marlene Sanders. That had started the sequence of events that brought me here, now, going to New Hampshire. I can only guess my intuition kicked in and I chose to follow it; and simply didn't pose those questions.

I did ask a lot of other questions though as my training progressed. What seemed to be my natural inclination was allowing me to practice watching, and listening, and interviewing.

There was other good news early on: two correspondents took exception to their peers' active avoidance of me.

Mal Goode was one of the two. The United Nations was his regular beat. And one day I was there with him and had a chance to get a good, close-up look and a feel for what it was like to be bigfooted on an assignment. The UN rarely made news of the sort that the big three networks covered. But in June of 1967 it was very much in the news as Israel battled Egypt in the Six-Day War. Despite the UN being his territory, Mal had to take a back seat to Lou Cioffi, ABC's international correspondent. Cioffi had covered the Korean and the Vietnam Wars, and it was decided by the powers in charge of ABC that the silver-haired Cioffi would handle the on-camera duties for all news coming from the UN about the Six-Day War. Maybe I was mistaken, but it seemed to me that Cioffi was sometimes a bit rattled doing his live cut-ins from the UN.

Laymond Robinson was the other correspondent. Tagging along on one of his assignments I got in touch with the kind of story I would love to do, if and when I ever got the chance. Laymond had set up an interview with Dorothy Maynor, an opera singer who in her retirement years had founded the Harlem School of the Arts. Maynor, unlike Marion Anderson whose story is widely known, was someone I knew nothing about. I had never heard of her or her school even though I lived in Harlem and thought I knew a lot about my community. I didn't ask Laymond how he knew of Maynor but he taught me an important lesson:

there were stories in my own backyard waiting to be told. I also didn't ask Laymond how he was able to convince the assignment desk to let him do a profile piece on a woman who ninety-nine percent of the ABC News audience had never heard of. What I did know from my time around the assignment desk was that it took self-confidence and salesmanship to successfully pitch a story about someone not in the limelight, but nonetheless interesting in their own right. This was the kind of insight not taught in journalism courses or books about reporting, but something one picked up from being around a man and a journalist like Laymond.

These two Black men—journalism professionals—allowed me, the news trainee, a look into their network-correspondents' world. And each in his own way encouraged me to stick things out when I became discouraged, when I worried that the internship was turning into a make-work project, leading nowhere. If either man had reservations about helping a "scab," answering her questions, allowing her to tag along with them, they never let on to me. Nor did they seem concerned about repercussions for taking me under their wings. I assumed that as Black men in the world of white male television journalists, they understood how it felt to be an outsider.

For his part, Mal was always outspoken about race. Laymond, on the other hand, never brought the subject up directly with me.

On the evening of June 4th, 1968, I happened to be working in the ABC News election unit and in the studio where Howard K. Smith had just wrapped up the network's coverage of the California Democratic presidential primary. Robert Kennedy had won it and delivered his victory speech.

Everyone thought we were finished for the night when word came across the Associated Press wire that Kennedy had been shot as he was leaving the Ambassador Hotel in downtown Los Angeles.

A ripple of disbelief spread through the studio. The election-unit producer immediately ordered the camera operators back to their places and told everyone else, me included, to stand by. On went the studio lights which had been shut down only moments ago. We went back on the air. Howard returned to his anchor desk with no script. He had only the AP report to go on and a few sketchy details as they began to come in. The details were few and they were grim.

Early the next day, Frank Mankiewicz, Kennedy's press secretary, his voice choked with emotion, announced that Kennedy was dead.

Arrangements were made for the New York senator's funeral at St. Patrick's Cathedral. Patrick Cardinal Cooke called a news conference to make them public and the network assignment-editor, fresh out of correspondents, spotted me and told me to go with the camera crew to St. Patrick's. He said I should take notes but stay out of the cameraman's way and if the cameraman asked me to carry his extra magazines of film (a non-union task), it was OK for me to do it. In other words, I should make myself useful and invisible at the same time.

The shock of Martin Luther King's assassination in Memphis in April and the riots it sparked still had a grip on my emotions as I did what I was told and hurried over to St. Patrick's. By now I was running on automatic, fueled in part by the caffeine from endless cups of coffee and the frenzied activity generated by the network assignment desk.

The following day, riding with the crew out to LaGuardia Airport, I felt I had moved up a step from news intern, though I had been given the same "help, but stay out of the way" instructions. At the airport I wedged myself into a spot alongside the TV news crews poised beside their heavy, black, tripod-mounted thirty-five-millimeter cameras and their boom microphones, and made myself look like I belonged with the network correspondents and other press from Washington and the White House who had come to New York from around the country and the world.

Before the body arrived, the reporters and correspondents talked among themselves in groups of two or three, looking worldly, self-assured, and very comfortable with each other, laughing when someone told a funny story, keeping their conversations low, and deep-voiced.

The plane landed smoothly, blowing its exhausts until its engines quieted and then it glided to a stop several hundred yards away from us. A black hearse slowly backed up and stopped close to the plane's rear cargo doors. A few minutes passed, then a crate holding Kennedy's casket was eased from the plane and lifted into the hearse as still cameras flashed, and television cameras recorded it all.

Just days after the Robert F. Kennedy assassination, I had the first indication someone besides my network bosses had noticed my internship. Ed Silverman, the news director of WABC-TV Channel 7, called me late one afternoon and said he wanted to see me.

"I wondered if you'd be interested in working for us," Ed asked once I was seated in his windowless, bargain-basement-furnished office. Ed was a genuine New Yorker who, except during his Army service, probably never set foot south of Atlantic City. A crooked smile formed by thin lips beneath a pencil-thin mustache and a face of high cheekbones gave him the appearance of a Mississippi riverboat gambler holding a handful of aces. I would later learn that indeed Ed and some of his male reporters did enjoy regular poker games after the five o'clock news program.

A week after that meeting with Ed—where I accepted his offer faster than fast—I moved from the network news offices at 66th Street and Central Park West to the Channel 7 office, up the block, at the corner of Columbus Avenue, and became the station's vacation-relief reporter. My temporary slot came with a cubicle near the men's bathroom and no guarantees. It was a big step up from network intern and a golden opportunity, my chance to break into local news.

15—Women and Minorities

Ain't I a Woman?

"Go get my purse, honey," began my mother's first arithmetic instructions to Connie and me. I knew she meant the worn workhorse of a leather handbag that she carried six days a week to her dry-cleaning job and not one of her fashionable clutch bags, the smart accessory she tucked under one arm on dress-up occasions.

From that big old everyday bag, she pulled out a zippered coin purse and dumped its contents—copper pennies, a few nickels and on some days a couple of dimes—clanging as they rolled out onto our Formica-topped kitchen table.

"Now if you move this penny, next to this penny, that makes two pennies," she would say, emphasizing "two," while slowly sliding the two coins off to one side of the table, "got that?" as she watched Connie and me nodding that her one-plus-one-equals-two example was now locked away in our heads. In the event one of us looked puzzled, she would do the one-penny-plus-one-penny-equals-two all over again. Once she was satisfied, she moved on. Whenever she decided Connie and I were ready, and she had some spare time between fixing dinner and leaving her girls to clean up the kitchen, my mother moved our arithmetic lessons up to the next level of double-digit addition and subtraction. And so it went. By the time my mother turned her rabbits over to the public school system, Connie and I had the arithmetic basics of addition and subtraction down cold.

Those early arithmetic lessons came in real handy much later when I was grown and realized how often people in big jobs, people running important businesses, had problems with numbers. More than once I have witnessed the sort of crazy-talk/stupid-talk that results when people who ought to know better fail to see that some of the things they say don't add up, when they conflate race and gender, or worse yet, when they ignore one and recognize the other, making someone invisible when maybe that person should be counted twice.

Here's a for-instance: Frank Bruni, a writer for the *New York Times*, in the Sunday, June 30, 2019 edition of the paper, was speculating on which of the Democrats would be a dream ticket to run for president and VP in 2020. Bruni wrote that five candidates in the large field were not the typical candidates: "Two of them are women, three are people of color."

Amy Klobuchar and Elizabeth Warren were his two women. Kamala Harris, Cory Booker and Julian Castro were his three people of color. So far, so good: two plus three equals five.

Of course, anybody paying attention knows that Harris *is* a woman, and not a *white* woman like Klobuchar and Warren. So that makes three women. And, Harris is one of Bruni's three people of color. So, based on my kitchen-table arithmetic, three women and three people of color adds up to six "top performers," as Bruni labeled them, not five. I know, this means counting Harris twice, both as a woman *and* a person of color.

It's also clear to me that Bruni's logic dictates that Harris cannot occupy *two* boxes. Somebody must choose. His privileged male whiteness grants him the power to decide which box she belongs in. And being someone with one of the big megaphones (the *New York Times),* he uses it to scratch Harris from the "women" category and assign her solely to the "people of color" lane. With his newspaper and other extraordinary ancillary access to the public conversation, Bruni influences the way ordinary, everyday newspaper-reading people will come to think, talk, and act. Those folks may, in fact, see no problem with the bad arithmetic; they may not even notice it.

But I can say this one thing with certainty: if Bruni had learned his numbers in the Susan Tolliver Kitchen-Table Arithmetic Course that says two plus three equals five, he would have passed. But he would have failed her Course in Common Sense. Furthermore, he would have had to explain to my mother how it is that a colored woman is not counted with the two white women? Ain't she a woman?

I witnessed another pathetic example of this sort of stupid-talk/crazy-talk on November 23rd, 1990, years after I had moved on from WABC-TV Eyewitness News and WNBC-TV NewsCenter 4, and was co-anchoring News 12 Long Island. The occasion was a panel discussion about the latest findings of "Women, Men, and Media," an annual survey conducted under the auspices of Columbia University and led by Betty Friedan, the high-profile feminist and *Feminine Mystique* author.

I had been invited to serve on a panel along with three other female journalists, two of them white, and Carole Simpson, a Black senior correspondent for ABC News at the time, and two white males, one a Public Television executive and the other, Max Frankel, executive editor of the *New York Times*.

At one point in the discussion, Frankel explained that if "a woman" working at the *Times* screwed up, she would be given one chance before he fired her. A Black reporter, on the other hand, would be allowed two screw-ups before they were let go. That's when I, a Black woman, piped up, "How many chances would I get to screw up if I worked at the *Times*?" Only Carole and I recognized the quicksand that Frankel had stepped into. Of course, he had no answer, because he didn't see the nuttiness of his remark, indeed of his newspaper's policy if he was being truthful.

Unlike Carole, who said she felt demeaned that Frankel expected less from a Black reporter, I didn't see it that way. I didn't feel demeaned at all. I understood Frankel to be saying that in his mind, "a woman" meant a white woman. And "a Black" meant any Black reporter, man or woman. Frankel didn't see how he mixed race and gender together. And according to his logic, I should be granted three screw-ups: one for being "a woman," and two more for being "a Black."

I found Frankel's comment both amusing and shameful. And I was somewhat surprised that all of the white panelists looked at me like I was nuts because I questioned the logic of his calculations.

When the panel broke for lunch, the others avoided me like the plague. But that was just as well, a bunch of young white students who had been in the audience and understood what they'd just seen and heard, welcomed me to talk with them about TV news and my rebuttal of Frankel.

Back at my office, I called Frankel at the *Times*, got his secretary, gave her my name to remind her boss of who I was, and said I wanted to invite him to lunch. She put me on hold, came back to the phone and said Mr. Frankel declined. "He's said all he has to say about the panel discussion."

That was 1990. Nearly two decades later, in 2008, *Newsweek* magazine, on a cover featuring headshots of Barak Obama and Hillary Clinton, posed the question: "Is America ready for a Black or a woman president?" Was the magazine talking race or gender? Or both at the same time? Why did the magazine fail to describe Obama as a Black *man* and Hillary as a *white* woman? Was *Newsweek* simply throwing equivalency out the window as it ignorantly discounted Obama's gender and Hillary's race?

In the mid-1960's the American vocabulary underwent a change and gained a new catchphrase: "women and minorities," three words which I call verbal shorthand. What the speaker of that phrase is really saying: *white* women and all those other folks. Or to be even more precise, "women and minorities" means *everybody but white men.*

Credit (or blame) for the genesis of that catchphrase might arguably be traced to Howard W. Smith. Howard W. Smith, a man I had somehow missed reading about in the newspapers or seeing on TV, was a longtime Democratic Congressman from Virginia, a white, eighty-year-old segregationist, and a fierce opponent of federal civil rights legislation.

Howard W. Smith was not just any member of the House of Representatives. He chaired the House Rules Committee where he had the power to stop or stall any legislation he didn't like. A top target became the civil rights bill fashioned by President Kennedy before he was murdered, then taken up by Lyndon Johnson when he assumed the Oval Office.

And depending on which version of history you buy, Smith used his power to contrive an amendment to the proposed legislation that would serve as a poison pill, in other words making it unpalatable to the bill's supporters and killing the entire legislation. At the same time Smith could use his amendment to curry favor with Alice Paul, leader of the National Women's Party and its constituency of white women. Or, as Smith is reported to have said later, "I'll tell you the truth. I offered it as a joke."

The *it* was a one-word amendment to Title VII, that part of the Civil Rights Act banning job discrimination based on race, color, religion, and national origin. And the one word was S-E-X.

For, as Smith saw it, the banning of discrimination based on race protected Black people (both men and women), but not white women. Smith's remedy was to insert in the law the word "sex" after the word religion. And if his "sex" amendment became part of Title VII, it would make white women a protected class right along with non-whites. The effect of adding "sex" to the Title VII language didn't simply help white women, it invented "two-fers" a derogatory label for women like me who are both Black (or non-white) and female, though most legislators apparently didn't see that at the time.

If Smith hoped that supporters of the Civil Rights Bill couldn't stomach his amendment and thus reject the entire legislation, his move backfired. After some delays, the bill passed the House with his amendment intact. It went on to the Senate, where white Southern Democrats stalled it for two months by organizing the longest filibuster in Senate history.

Finally, in July, the 1964 Civil Rights Act, including the amended Title VII, was passed and signed into law.

A year later, with the Equal Employment Opportunities Commission (EEOC) established to administer the law, women were made a "protected class." And a few years later, the Federal Communications Commission (FCC) adopted a rule change to have women counted as "minorities" in the awarding, renewing, or denying of broadcast licenses. In neither instance did the EEOC or the FCC make it explicit that since non-white women are counted as *minorities*, the *women* being protected by the regulatory agencies must be *white women*. Unless, of course they were counting a non-white woman twice, as a minority *and* as a woman.

This, despite the obvious fact that in American parlance, minorities means non–white racial and ethnic groups. And equally obvious is the fact that *men, children,* **and** *women* comprise these non-white groups.

And so, the diabolical and misleading language of "women and minorities" entered the lexicon.

I don't know if, in 1967, the ABC brass had in mind to appease the broadcast licensing gods of the Federal Communications Commission when they created a news-trainee program and offered me the chance to be the guinea pig for it. Perhaps they did, but I didn't ask if their move was a chance to check off two boxes: woman (check), minority (check).

The tension between advocates of civil rights for all Black people and advocates for white women's rights has a long history, dating as far back as the Fourteenth Amendment granting Black men (when only males had the franchise) the right to vote after the Thirteenth Amendment abolishing slavery.

I did know that in 1963 when Betty Friedan's *The Feminine Mystique* was published and became a best-seller, her book was not about me. Friedan wasn't speaking for or about me or any consequential women in my world. Friedan's commiserating was with white suburban wives who chose lives as homemakers over careerists and then felt miserable about their choices. Indeed, the "large population of middle-aged women who had no children left at home, no particular need to work for money, no household chores that were demanding, and decades of life still ahead of them," as former *New York Times* editorial writer Gail Collins described Friedan's subjects, were foreign to me.

Sojourner Truth had faced that issue head on and in everyday language at a Women's Rights Conference in my hometown of Akron, Ohio in 1851. When some at that conference sought to define womanhood on their terms, Sojourner Truth was quick to challenge them. "Ain't I a woman?" asked the former slave, turned abolitionist and advocate of full rights for all women, not just women who she said got helped into carriages, lifted over mud puddles, and given the best places—in other words, white women whose lives and experiences were not Sojourner Truth's. She let them know that she had ploughed and planted, worked as hard and ate as much as any man, bore the lash as well, birthed thirteen children and had no one but Jesus to share her mother's grief when most of her offspring were sold into slavery. I only wish I could have been around back then to give a shout out and a couple of amens to Sojourner Truth.

Her "Ain't I a woman?" question is still alive and well nearly a dozen decades later.

Other new language introduced in the 50's and 60's to talk about women, white people, and Black folks—particularly in employment—emerged as both policy descriptions and prescriptions for dealing with racial and gender inequities. One of those was "affirmative action."

In my experience "affirmative action" became a loaded term, insinuating that Black folks are getting an undeserved, unwarranted break. People who talk about the beneficiaries of affirmative action may have in their minds an image of the blond and white Lesley Stahl of CBS News and 60 Minutes fame. But I doubt it. Though Stahl herself has said that she, a white woman, Connie Chung of Asian background, and Bernie Shaw, a Black man, all hired by CBS in 1972, were, in her words, "affirmative action babies."

I wonder how this linguistic nonsense-salad would be sorted out around the kitchen table of Susan Tolliver's Course in Common Sense?

16—Dead Last

And some of them were also journalists.

Under Ed Silverman, WABC-TV Channel 7 ranked dead last in the news program ratings, way behind its main competitors, WCBS-TV Channel 2 and WNBC-TV Channel 4, the other network flagship stations. Even the independently owned station WOR-TV Channel 9 ate our lunch. Around the city—and even in the Channel 7 newsroom—people joked that our own relatives wouldn't be caught watching us.

The Silverman-directed news staff could best be described as a hodgepodge of personalities, some of whom were also journalists: John Parsons, a red-headed, pudgy Italian who'd undergone a last-name change from Pedillo; gossip columnist Cindy Adams of the immovable piled-high hair and spouse of comedian Joey Adams; Gil Noble, tall, dark and handsome jazz pianist turned reporter and one of the early Black TV news hires who Channel 7 hired while I was in training up the block at the network news; Betty Adams, a white middle-aged writer whose face showed plenty of wear and who knew her stuff; Milton Lewis, a tiny man with an encyclopedic knowledge of New York City politics dating back to the wheeling, dealing days of Tammany Hall and who made "Now listen to this" his reporting signature; Betsy Aaron, a youngish white woman generally regarded as a serious journalist who eagerly

ditched the local station when ABC network news offered
her a slot as a correspondent; Howard Cosell, the toupee-
wearing, cigar-smoking former lawyer turned sports
commentator, who loved to show off his amazing ability to
deliver an on-camera, unscripted, perfectly-timed
monologue without a hitch; and Jimmy Breslin, gregarious
Irishman and popular columnist for the tabloid *New York
Daily News,* who came across ill at ease on TV, reading his
columns filled with colorful quotes from equally colorful
characters (some of whom his critics said were made up),
and which some of his fans said were reminiscent of Damon
Runyon, the iconic newsman and chronicler of New York
City life.

Silverman and his assignment-desk editors wasted no
time throwing me into this mix. I went out on stories with
film crews every day. On one of my earliest assignments, I
was sent with a film crew to lower Manhattan, where huge
construction vehicles and muscle-bound men in hard hats
noisily worked around a huge hole in the ground. From that
spot the first of the World Trade Center twin towers would
one day rise.

Back in the office, with the film from that shoot,
dispatched from the film lab to one of the small, dimly-lit
editing rooms, I watched over the film editor's shoulder as
he spliced together the pictures (called B-roll) that would
help tell my story when he synched it up with my
narration/voiceover (called A-roll) on a second track. The
first time I heard my disembodied voice waft into the room,
I felt sick to my stomach. Surely that slooooooow taaaalking,
soft-as-a-baby's-behind sound couldn't really be me, could
it? Maybe the sound man on my camera crew had fiddled

with the dials on his equipment, playing a practical joke on this newbie.

But yes, the voice that bore no resemblance to how I *thought* I sounded, or ought to sound, *was* me. And it took a while to get used to that fact. Just like my sweaty palms, my slight hand tremor and my shiny nose, the voice was mine, part of the package. The package that would get sent out to cover fires, funerals, press conferences, protests, lost pets, and busted water mains: the bread and butter of local news stations everywhere, including the five boroughs of New York City and the two neighboring states of New Jersey and Connecticut. My assignments were the kind typically given to women.

Channel 7, smallest of the local broadcast stations owned and operated by the three networks (called O&O's), was always undermanned, so anything the senior male reporters were too busy to do, or simply didn't want to do, I did.

I learned on the fly how to write "standups," that's TV lingo for the stories I composed while out in the field on location. Armed with paper and pen (and trusty tape recorder for preserving interview sound-bites), I wrote the beginnings and endings (called opens and closes) of my standup scripts, then memorized and recorded it all on-camera. At the same time, I directed the cameraman of my three-man crew, which included a lighting and sound person (all of them men), making sure that we were all on the same page about the shots I wanted for my story. Once I had the on-camera part of the standup "in the can," I wrote the off-camera narration part of the story. And I wrote wherever I could: on location where the story happened, or in the crew car en route to my next assignment, or back in the office.

Each standup required me to be the actor, director, and producer of a mini-movie, making coherent the on- and off-camera narration, the sound bites from recorded interviews and other relevant pieces. Weaving all these elements together under the pressure of deadlines and time slots dictated by the show producers was, for me, the most difficult and demanding part of street reporting.

Paying attention to film editors and cameramen at work and asking lots of questions, I learned what pictures made the best film sequences, and tried to be mindful of the well-worn TV dictum to "show, don't tell."

As my vacation-relief tryout was ending, Silverman thought enough of my work to sign me to a full-time, three-year contract. He did so just before the men in the executive suites fired him in September and hired a new news director, Al Primo.

Al Primo was coming from Philadelphia to save us. KYW-TV, part of the Westinghouse Group and Primo's previous station, had been a loser before he implemented his *Eyewitness News* format and turned that station's news operation around, making it number one in its market. Leonard Goldenson, chairman of ABC, and other top brass were counting on Primo to do the same for us and their flagship's laughingstock news operation.

I didn't know what to expect from the new guy. If he came in looking to clean house, as expected, he might logically begin with me. On the other hand, maybe I wouldn't be on his hit list since I earned the lowest salary, didn't complain out loud about it, and was eager for assignments.

Prior to Primo's arrival, intense speculation fueled by rumors of drastic changes ahead had me expecting a ferocious, fire-breathing ogre roaring into the newsroom, clutching a whip with one gnarly hand and a hit list in the other. Primo was no ogre. He was no creampuff, either.

A proud Italian from hardscrabble Pittsburgh, Primo had worked his way up into the middle class. He brought an air of intense, quiet energy to the newsroom. He smoked a pipe, sometimes clenched just a bit too tightly between his perfect, white teeth.

When the pipe wasn't in his mouth, he was cleaning it or filling it with tobacco from a dark brown leather pouch. Primo was good looking, too. The bit of grey at his temples in his otherwise jet-black hair gave him a mature, distinguished appearance.

Primo didn't get rid of me. It was only a matter of a few months however, before he changed everything about our news program.

17—The Primo Effect

We're going to call it Eyewitness News

Al Primo, godfather to the eyewitness concept of local news reporting, gave a new face and brought a new name to TV news in the New York market. That is, he was finding news outside the usual sources and hiring as reporters, folks who knew where to find those sources.

He charged the anchors. Breaking with tradition, he jettisoned the solo anchorman and installed co-anchors. He replaced our matinee idol anchor, John Schubeck, with Roger Grimsby. And after a few trials with other deep-voiced white males with chiseled features, he paired the acerbic, quick-witted Roger Grimsby with Bill Beutel, a mild-mannered, "Mr. Nice Guy," a product of Cleveland, Ohio, and ABC's London bureau, who told corny jokes and was often the butt of Grimsby's iconoclastic humor.

Our West 66th Street studio got a makeover. Out went the old standard-issue set, replaced by a more modern-looking tiered platform. Not satisfied with the program's opening shot, Primo choreographed a new one, trademarked by having his street reporters walking onto the set from off-camera and taking seats behind one of the desks on the raised platforms. In what had always been the domain of the news anchors—the studio—we street reporters opened and closed our filmed stories live and on camera and were given a few extra seconds after our reports to chat briefly with Roger and Bill.

Primo ordered a new musical opening for the show and chose the soundtrack from the Steve McQueen and Paul Newman movie, *Cool Hand Luke.*

Roger Sharpe, Doug Johnson, Milt Lewis, Duke Wade, Bob Miller, Bill Aylward, and Bob Lape (who like me had grown up in Akron and attended Buchtel High at the same time as my best friend, Martha) were some of the reporters Primo either inherited or he himself hired. They all had impressive resumes and looked to Primo like they could cut it as "eyewitnesses." And with one exception, they were all white males. The exception, Gil Noble, had been hired by Primo's predecessor, the same news director who hired me just before he himself was axed.

Born and raised in Harlem, Gil studied at City College, played jazz piano and aspired to be the next Erroll Garner, all the while working part time as an announcer for WLIB, a Black-audience-oriented radio station where he gained newsroom experience and chose a different career path. In 1967, at the height of "the long hot summer," Gil successfully auditioned for a reporting job with WABC-TV.

Ed Silverman, the news director, soon expanded Gil's reporting duties and made him a weekend anchor. And when Robert Hooks, the actor and first host of *Like It Is,* WABC-TV's Black-issues-oriented public-affairs program, moved on, Gil was tapped to replace him.

Primo added yet another ethnic dimension to his lineup in 1970 when he hired Geraldo Rivera, son of a Jewish mother and Puerto Rican father. Rivera, with his mustachioed street-swagger not only looked the part of a credible eyewitness, he had gained notoriety as an anti-establishment lawyer who counted among his clients the political activist, confrontational, purple-beret-wearing Young Lords. At Primo's urging, Rivera (allegedly also known as Gerry Rivers at one point in his college career) agreed to acquire some formal news-reporter training in the Summer Program for Minority Journalists, a Kerner Commission-inspired industry initiative headquartered at Columbia University's Graduate School of Journalism. Geraldo would fill a spot sponsored by the station, and while he did join the program, I doubt Geraldo ever thought he actually needed any training.

Later on, looking to add one of his own to *Eyewitness News,* Primo lured fellow Italian, Rosanne Scamardella, away from New York City's Human Rights Commission. Around that time Primo also raided a competing station—WCBS-TV Channel 2—to bring on board Gloria Rojas, the Puerto Rican woman who had originally recommended Geraldo to Primo.

Primo outfitted the male reporters in dark-blue blazers with the number 7 gold-stitched and encircled on the breast pockets. Primo even dressed up our street microphones, adding the new number 7 logo to the mic tags, in yet another move to distance Channel 7 *Eyewitness News* from the competition.

Primo did something else that just about destroyed Tex Antoine, the weatherman. He bumped off Uncle Wethbee, Antoine's longtime prop and partner, a cartoon character affectionately known as "Unk." Before each news program, Tex donned a blue artist's smock and drew Unk anew, reflecting the day's weather in Unk's facial expressions and in his dress. Unk's demise cast a temporary pall over the weather reports.

Primo broke even more conventions when he commissioned a slew of TV commercials and newspaper ads as part of his campaign to raise our ratings by attracting new viewers and seducing some of our competitor's audiences. The advertising featured both news anchors, a couple of sports guys, the weatherman, a select few reporters—all of them white men—and me, the Black female.

One TV commercial, shot in Central Park, had co-anchors, Grimsby and Beutel, playing football with me and two of the sports guys, Frank Gifford, the former New York Giants halfback, and Jim Bouton, the ex-Yankees pitcher who authored *Ball Four,* a tell-all book that made Bouton *persona non grata* with the Yankee organization and his former teammates.

Perhaps the most memorable of those TV spots showed a bunch of us crashing a make-believe Puerto Rican wedding with Geraldo introducing us—one by one—to a roomful of guests, followed by scenes of everybody dancing to lively music and having a high old time. The idea was to show the *Eyewitness News* team as one big happy family that fit in with our neighbors. The commercials proved controversial. They also worked. They enticed people into watching our news program. And for many of those people ours became their program of choice. As a 1973 *New York Times* profile observed, *Eyewitness News* became a fixture in the living rooms, bedrooms, or kitchens of almost a million viewers every night.

In 1956, when I first moved to New York to go to Bellevue, I found it odd that everybody referred to Manhattan as "the city." It was as if the Bronx, Brooklyn, Queens, and Staten Island were separate cities, not parts of the Big Apple. And in the minds of many, they were and still are "the outer boroughs."

The first time I set foot on Staten Island as a reporter, I could see why folks living there felt disconnected from "the city" of concrete sidewalks and steel skyscrapers. Their bit of New York—with all the open areas of former farmland—looked like it had been picked up somewhere in the Midwest and dropped into New York Harbor. The news desk had sent me to interview John Marchi, a Republican state senator who was trying to become mayor of New York (all of it.) Marchi, born and bred on Staten Island, was deeply Italian, like most of his fellow residents. And I wondered if any of them had rubbed shoulders with a Black person, much less been interviewed by one. Nevertheless, the interview went well, Marchi and his family were gracious, and I had a bit of fun in my piece playing with the fact that Marchi lived on Victory Boulevard. He lost his mayoral bid, in 1969 and again in 1973, but apparently never lost his campaign to cut ties with "the city" and make Staten Island, its smallest, least populated borough, a separate city.

Not long after my introduction to Staten Island, I was assigned to cover yet another mayoral candidate, this one in Brooklyn, the biggest of New York City's boroughs and the one with the most people. Pulling up to one of those iconic brownstones in Brooklyn Heights with my crew, I couldn't get over the irony of being assigned to interview one of its more famous and notorious residents, the writer Norman Mailer, not as an author, but because he was running for mayor of New York in 1969. His running mate, vying for City Council president, was the writer and tabloid- newspaper columnist, Jimmy Breslin. Like Marchi, these two scribes wanted to reshape New York City (all of it), but they had in mind a grander secession scheme: they wanted to turn New York City into the fifty-first state.

Because of my experience as a features reporter, I was picked to co-host a pre-taped program that aired in the National Football League's 1970 season just ahead of ABC network's *Monday Night Football*. Produced by Channel 7, the network's local station, and hosted by former players Frank Gifford, the Giants halfback, and Don Meredith, the Dallas Cowboys quarterback, our show consisted of insider-football stuff, star-player interviews with folks like Fran Tarkenton, the Giants and Vikings hall-of-famer, whose wife had penned a book for women demystifying downs and plays and other intricacies of football. I had fun doing that show and displaying some of the football knowledge I had gained watching the Cleveland Browns with my best girlfriend and her four brothers, and being a cheerleader watching my own high school teams play in Akron's Rubber Bowl on Friday nights and Thanksgiving Days.

Our local-station pre-game TV show had a short life, lasting only one season before it got sent to the showers. Our small-potatoes program was no match for Roone Arledge, creator of *Monday Night Football* and legendary sports producer, who succeeded in making strange bedfellows of Gifford, Meredith and Howard Cosell share one broadcast booth.

But before our little show ran its course, I got to shoot a profile of the Washington Redskins marching band that allowed me a trip out of town and the chance to walk on a regulation football field. And because Ed "the Flea" Bell, the Jets wide receiver who wore Number 7 on his jersey, size-wise was not all that much bigger than me, I tried my hand at comedy by raiding the Jets locker room and suiting up in Bell's uniform and helmet.

George Blanda made my list of interview subjects, too. The record-holder for kicking extra points at that time, Blanda was in New York for a game and staying at the Summit Hotel in Manhattan. Instead of letting me and my camera crew come up to his room for the interview, he met us in the hotel lobby. It was only years later, when male celebrities were making unwanted news, accused of making unwanted sexual advances, that it occurred to me that Blanda was making sure his room was out of bounds to female reporters, even one accompanied by a three-man camera crew.

Primo loved to do the unexpected. If a story allowed for a perspective different from what our audience was accustomed to, or if it called for sending a reporter out of town because Primo or one of the show producers saw a news connection to our local area and they thought the story would grab our viewers, he turned his reporter loose. And I often benefited.

One baseball season, Primo sent me to Florida instead of the regular sports guy, to cover the Yankees and Mets in their spring training camps. I had never been to Florida, nor reported on baseball. Growing up among rabid fans of the Cleveland Indians and having seen Satchel Paige and Larry Doby in action was as close as I had come to that assignment, which challenged me to learn a lot, fast. Among other things, I was pressed to know the rosters of both teams, the correct baseball terminology, and how to deal with some of the staff who worried that my tender ears might be offended by some of the locker-room language of his players, or that my moderately high heels might get caught in the turf.

I wrote my training-camp standups whenever I found a place to perch. One time, that happened to be in the stands just behind the catcher's spot. A batter practicing his swing knocked a ball into the stands where I sat scribbling and deciphering my notes. I ducked and just missed getting conked in the head.

In one report I described "a passed ball," and got a letter from a fan saying there is no such thing. Maybe he was just testing me, but I was right, there is such a thing.

In addition to the linguistic homeruns and errors, the baseball assignment showed me what it takes to be on your own on the road in unfamiliar settings. Just me to line up interviews, write my scripts and standups, and arrange to ship my film back to New York to be edited and aired.

In March 1973, Primo agreed to send me to Hollywood to cover the Academy Awards. For the first time in Academy history, the five nominees in the best actress category included not one, but two black actresses: Cicely Tyson for *Sounder* and Diana Ross for *Lady Sings the Blues*.

I had previously interviewed both women before their nominations were announced. And I argued that *Eyewitness News* ought to be at the Oscars to capture the historic moment if either of them won. Cicely or Diana walking away with an Oscar would be a natural follow-up to my one-on-ones with them. And what could be better than having a hometown reporter break down the glitz and glamour of Tinsel Town's biggest night of the year? Our coverage would be another feather in *Eyewitness News's* cap. Our viewers would love it. Plus, the movie version of *Cabaret,* the Broadway blockbuster, had a shot at garnering a couple of golden statues, giving the assignment yet another New York angle. All that sealed the deal and Primo sent me to Hollywood.

It was a "mostly on your own" assignment again, one that required me to be the reporter as well as field producer, writer, and interviewer. Working with a Los Angeles-based local station cameraman who I was meeting for the first time, I directed him to shoot all the background stuff before he and I and his sound and lighting guys all sped over to the Dorothy Chandler Pavilion. Outside the theatre, I polled some of the cheering, hyped-up movie fans waiting behind the barricades as the celebrities arrived, all dolled up and striking poses for the still photographers and TV cameramen. We captured the madness on film in the usual "eyewitness" style. When Diana arrived, I pulled her aside for a quick interview and told her that based on my unofficial poll, she was a shoo-in to win best actress. And, having won the Foreign Press trophy handed out a few days earlier, she possibly had reason to believe me. But my prediction skills, unfortunately, turned out to be nonexistent. Liza Minnelli won.

The evening's highlight though, was not Diana's documented and devastating meltdown when she lost, but Marlon Brando's boycott of the ceremony. Nominated as best actor for his performance as Vito Corleone in *The Godfather,* Brando snubbed the Academy and sent Princess Sacheen Littlefeather, a Native American woman, in his stead. She gracefully, and on Brando's instructions, refused his best actor statue. Her non-acceptance speech protested the movie portrayals of American Indians and called attention to the long-running standoff of Indian activists at Wounded Knee.

On the red-eye back to New York, I stayed awake, wading through my notes, writing my piece, safeguarding my film, and praying that once I got back to the office, Marty Berman, the very talented young Jewish film editor who adored Johnny Mathis tunes and spliced film together as if he were composing a piece of music, would be free to edit my Oscars story. Luckily, he was. I handed over my pre-recorded narration track with its sound bites indicated and left to cool my heels at McGlade's, the bar across the street from our office and a favorite between-shows hangout of the male staff. Never a real drinker, I ordered a stiff one on the rocks, maybe a Johnny Walker Black, the only drink I knew by name.

Back in Marty's editing room, peering over his shoulder as he showed me the finished piece, he whispered, "Is that alcohol I smell on your breath?"

"Yep," I confessed. I thought I deserved it, needed it to keep myself together for the six and eleven. Except for Marty, no one seemed the wiser that I had needed a drink to help me through the two programs. They had no idea the weight I felt lifted after the I left the studio that night. The relief that I had done what I would have considered impossible just days before.

From my earliest assignment (reporting the beginning of construction on the World Trade Center towers) to my last WABC report (a half hour profile of Gordon Parks, the groundbreaking photojournalist and filmmaker), my news career had mostly been that of general assignment reporter. Meaning, I had no regular beat, no specialty based on expertise or experience, I was not primarily responsible for reporting and/or breaking stories about education, politics, police and so on. Instead, I simply showed up every day and got sent on whatever scheduled happenings or breaking news the assignment-desk editor thought our station needed to cover—transit strike, busted water-main, four-alarm fire, drug bust, bank robbery, hostage-taking, anti-Vietnam-War protests, teacher strikes, women's-lib demonstrations, Black Panther school breakfasts, fashion shows, and more.

Over time, as I gained experience and showed interest in, and a willingness to take on, other kinds of assignments, I served as co-anchor and associate producer of the Sunday evening news program. I co-hosted *Like It Is,* a Black-issues-oriented public affairs program. For a time, I also co-hosted *A.M. New York* with Dan Daniels, a popular radio DJ, after John Bartholomew Tucker left. That program required a radical change in my sleep schedule. Ordinarily not an early riser, I had to be up before dawn and in the studio by 5am. Among our notable guests, Congresswoman Shirley Chisholm who was then campaigning to become US President (years later, I would interview her for a long article in *Good Housekeeping* magazine), also Ed Lewis, a publisher of *Essence,* a new magazine for Black women.

I hosted and reported for *People, Places, and Things,* a weekly magazine-format features series; and *Melba Tolliver's New York,* a one-off compilation of feature stories.

I can't pinpoint when or why it occurred to me that nobody was holding a gun to my head, nobody forcing me to report the news in exactly the same way as everyone else more experienced than me. I simply realized, over time, that I actually had choices, and that I had been making those choices, instinctively or intuitively. My stories had the relevant information, the "who" and the "what" were accurate, but after that I could take a few chances, depending on the situation. For instance, if a government official called a news conference and I saw that he was talking to a bunch of empty chairs, and not to the people most likely to be affected by his announcement of some new policy or program, I could show that we reporters and our camera crews were his only audience. Or, when reporting from a big celebrity event, I could make sure my cameraman shot footage of folks on the other side of the velvet ropes. And I could talk to those people, making them the main event and the celebrities the sidebars.

Clearly, I had an aversion to focusing only on the "big shots," something I had criticized in my 1963 letter to the *Herald Tribune*. And now that I was in a position to seek different perspectives from which to report news stories, I saw no good reason for me not to do so. I could choose to give viewers something unexpected, yet something they could relate to.

This was possible because I was reporting for *Eyewitness News*. It also helped that as a reporter for a local station in New York City, not in Cleveland or Milwaukee, I was working in the media capitol of the world, headquarters for all sorts of companies and institutions, the city through which all types of newsworthy characters passed and where local news ranked right up there with national news.

Before *Eyewitness News,* it seemed to me that except for the occasional "MOS"—shorthand for "man on the street"—sound bites, the big shots were allowed to hog the spotlight in most news stories. I watched that begin to change after Al Primo brought his *Eyewitness News* philosophy to Channel 7. And it seemed to me that his philosophy and my instinct to see issues of the day from the perspective of the everyday, ordinary people were a good fit. We seemed tailor made for each other.

It was a good sign, as Primo writes in his own book, *Eyewitness Newsman,* that when Rona Barrett, told him, "Nobody gives a shit about ordinary people," he rebuffed the Hollywood gossip columnist even though she was a fixture on the show *Roger Grimsby and the Noisemakers* before Primo took over. Plus, Rona had friends in the upper echelons of the ABC network. And when "Miss Rona," as Grimsby liked to call her, locked horns with Primo, she threatened to take her complaints about him to his bosses. She ended up the loser in that battle. Primo cut ties with Miss Rona, telling her that *Eyewitness News* was going to be television's first people-oriented news program about regular people, the ones she so detested, and not the celebrities she knew so well. With that it was curtains for Miss Rona.

Cutting ties with Miss Rona was just one of Primo's moves in his makeover on the way news would be done on Channel 7. The hiring of Howard Weinberg, a writer/producer who came over from public television, was another one, one that fit Primo's thinking that "people can tell their stories better than we can." With Howard producing, I was the reporter for *Consciousness Rising,* a program intended to translate some of the most commonly accepted feminist rhetoric into everyday reality, as lived by everyday women.

Around then, I went to management with an idea for an ongoing series that I wanted to create and call *Profiles.* They gave it the OK and I invited Howard to team up with me. *Profiles* became a popular series of mini documentaries, ranging in length from five to twelve minutes and featuring people who gave our region its character, but who were not your typical newsmakers. *Profiles* was based on the premise that at the core of every issue are the people most affected by it.

People who know me well, joke that "I wonder" is my standard way of starting most conversations. And being the reporter and face of *Profiles* gave me a chance to wonder out loud and on camera about all sorts of things. "I wonder what it's like to deal day after day with the mountain of garbage generated by eight-million New Yorkers?" Monty Piccioni answered that question when Howard and I followed him at work, first behind the wheel of a humongous Sanitation Department truck, and then trailed him home to Staten Island where we learned more about him and his family in familiar surroundings, mixing Q&A with Italian treats.

Anyone who watched construction on the World Trade Center twin towers, or a multi-story apartment building, may have glanced to the heavens and wondered as I did, about the tiny figures, miles above the ground creating the buildings' steel skeletons. Roger Littlehorn, Mohawk Indian, described what it's like to be a—in his words—"skywalker," and sort out the truth of American Indians excelling as steelworkers, and a lot more, for *Profiles*.

It's a given that talented boy athletes can make names for themselves and go on to college on scholarships. Why not the same for girls, and who, if anyone, is trying to even the playing field? I wondered. Few people living outside Brooklyn knew of Fred Thompson, corporate lawyer, founder in 1963 of the all-girls Atoms Track Club, and its coach. Even after one of Thompson's kids, Cheryl Toussaint, representing the United States in the 1972 Olympics, ran the sixteen-hundred-meter relay and brought home a silver medal, the Atoms's celebrity remained mostly in the neighborhood. That changed after a million pairs of eyes watching *Profiles* on *Eyewitness News* met the kids and the coach. Those viewers also learned that Thompson measured his runners' success not by medals but by graduations from high school and college. Thompson's own experience growing up in Bedford Stuyvesant, the heart of Black Brooklyn, honed that belief, as well as his determination that girl athletes have parity with boys. The saying "It's not who you know, but who knows you," had the ring of truth when Colgate-Palmolive executives found out about Thompson from our TV profile. They saw him as a worthy partner and gave their name to his efforts as sponsors of the Colgate Women's Games and scholarships for girls and women. Thompson was named director of the games, which debuted in 1974, drawing female runners from all around the East Coast, not just Brooklyn. By the time of Thompson's death in 2019, he had been inducted into the USA Track and Field Hall of Fame. And Toussaint has succeeded him as director of the Colgate Games.

Another of our *Profiles* subjects, New Jersey housewife Mary Alice Yurica, married to a business executive, and mother of three school-age children, personified the real-life consequences and challenges one stay-at-home mom faced when she chose to put her college degree to use and join the nine-to-five work force, acting on the rhetoric of the women's movement. Howard and I showed in this profile that for this woman—and countless others like her—such a decision would take some doing and result in unexpected consequences when the rhetoric hit the road. Post-its and schedules covered the front of her refrigerator reminding which kid had to be where at what time and what day of the week. The woman found only a part-time job that could accommodate her domestic and parental commitments.

Our list of *Profiles* mixed lots of folks, some of them even celebrities: Ted Kheel, labor lawyer and contract negotiator; Douglas Leigh, the man responsible for many of the memorable billboards above Times Square; Rene Dubos, French-American microbiologist and Pulitzer-Prize-winning author of *So Human an Animal*.

I was proud of *Profiles*, personally and professionally. It re-affirmed my belief, and what I admit is my consciously-arrived-at personal and professional worldview, that everyday ordinary folks have stories to tell and deserve to tell them on TV where millions of people can learn something about someone or something they previously knew nothing about. I hoped each viewer would watch my segment and come away thinking or saying, "I didn't know that." Or, "I never thought about it that way before." *Profiles* was a winner, but this program breathed its last when cigarette advertising was pulled from TV, resulting in budget cuts.

In 1973, the ABC TV network created *Americans All,* a *Profiles*-like show for its national audience. "We wanted to try something more serious—" said the vice president for documentaries in a December 14th, 1973 *Washington Post* article. Explaining the genesis of a programming alternative to the promotional time-slot fillers that followed the Sunday-night movies, he said, "—and we decided on a vehicle that would not only share the contributions of minorities to the fabric of America, but give our minority employees a chance to research, produce, and handle something on their way to bigger things with the network." Four staffers, three of them Black females, were assigned to the program. On the list of subjects for the first year of the program, according to *Americans All* associate producer, Willie Catherine Suggs, were eight Black topics or individuals, three Spanish-speaking people, and one American Indian. I served as the on-camera narrator/interviewer for films featuring Alvin Ailey, Black choreographer and founder of his American Dance Theatre; Roberto Mondragon, Chicano Lieutenant Governor of New Mexico; Tom Bradley, Black mayor of Los Angeles; and Brock Peters and Vinnette Carroll, Black actors reading the works of Langston Hughes. Other films featured Harry Low, a Chinese-American judge and political figure; and Norman Mineta, a Japanese-American congressman, both Californians; and Vine Deloria, Standing Sioux theologian, and author of *Custer Died for Your Sins*. Working on *Americans All* was for me a welcome opportunity to travel, interview and learn from a variety of folks from different backgrounds and cultures. But unlike *Profiles*, they were not the everyday, ordinary folks I generally tended to cover.

Near the end of my time with *Eyewitness News,* I was tapped to co-anchor the Sunday 5pm news with Doug Johnson. That's when I asked for and got a show credit as associate producer. It was mid-morning on one of those Sundays, June 30th, 1974, and I was in our newsroom, involved in early preparations for our early evening program. So far, it was turning out to be what we call in the news business a slow news day. Just another pretty, quiet summer day, not much going on in the tri-state region covered by our local station.

Out of the blue that changed. A bulletin came across the clattering AP wire machine. And someone yelled out "Hey, heads up." What happened next was silence. Quickly followed by disbelief. "What? Are you sure? Let me see that." Those of us closest to the assignment desk and the wire-copy machine crowded around, read the news out loud: some eight-hundred-miles away, in Atlanta, Georgia, the mother of Martin Luther King, Jr. had been killed. Shot to death in her church, Ebenezer Baptist. As she sat at a new organ playing the opening strains of "The Lord's Prayer," a visitor rose up from a pew close by her, pulled out two pistols and started shooting. When the shooting stopped Mrs. King, seventy, and Edward Boykin, sixty-nine, a church deacon, were dead. At least one other church member was injured. Martin Luther King, Sr. had been the gunman's real target.

But Mrs. King had been in closer range to the shooter and so the elder King had been spared.

The shooter, Marcus Wayne Chenault, was not from Atlanta. He had traveled there from Ohio. Members of Ebenezer had welcomed the stranger to their Sunday morning service, doing what their faith and Bible taught them to do.

One could not escape the irony: a mother whose son was shot to death in Memphis six years earlier while planning a protest in support of sanitation workers. Both murdered as they worked for causes greater than themselves. My mind was a jumble. Until one thought forced its way to the forefront. Who in our local area knew Alberta King? Who could help me report this horrible event to the viewers who would tune in to our news in a few hours?

In the days before the Internet and Facebook and all the other social media and instant everything, there was the telephone, the clumsy contraption that you picked up and dialed the number of the person you wanted to speak to. That person was the Reverend Wyatt Tee Walker, pastor at New Canaan Baptist Church in Harlem. He was just ending his own Sunday morning service when I reached him. He was by then aware of the news about Mrs. King and he agreed to be interviewed. I can't quote Reverend Walker's exact words. I can only recall his grief, and his calm, comforting demeanor as he recalled Alberta King and his years as chief-of-staff and confidante to her son, in his role as an early strategist for the civil-rights protests led by the Southern Christian Leadership Conference. That interview set the tone for our program that afternoon and was a gift to our audience. Unlike her martyred son, Alberta King never gained world-wide fame, was never awarded a peace prize, never memorialized with a statue in the nation's capital, never honored with a national holiday in her name.

No, Alberta King was one of those everyday people, like so many I knew and who helped raise me. She may simply have been what is every mother's dream: to be a woman, in her case a Black woman, who births and raises a child who makes her proud.

On another one of those slow-news-day Sundays, a wire service story caught my eye. It described a suburban Westchester college just outside New York City that was offering a course in Peace Studies. Peace Studies, I thought. Never heard of that. Wonder what that could be. The next week, I started to find out, after convincing the assignment editor that a Peace Studies story would be something different for the next Sunday. Working on that story taught me a few things: stick a microphone in the face of your average New Yorker and ask, "What's your definition of peace?" and chances are good they'll think you're playing a prank on them. Those who play along will struggle a bit before saying something they hope makes sense. And most will finally offer some version of, "Peace is the absence of war." With the best of these so-called "man-on-the-street" responses, I began to build my piece, along with an interview with the professor teaching that Westchester college program. Next, I gathered some clips of the two Irish women peace activists Betty Williams and Mai read Corrigan, co-recipients of the 1976 Nobel Peace Prize for their organizing and promoting to end the "troubles" in Northern Ireland.

So far, my piece was all talking heads—good and appropriate as they were—still talking heads. And that taught me that it's hard to visualize peace for the visual medium of TV. Peace marches and protest signs? White doves? Fingers in the peace sign? T-shirts? Bumper stickers?

On the other hand, war images are a dime a dozen. War and combat are also embedded in our talk. War on drugs. Fighting cancer. Fighting for justice. Fighting for equality. Fighting for the White House ... on and on.

So, lessons learned, some topics simply make for better TV than others. I cobbled together my piece on peace, aired it on the next Sunday program, and moved on.

Al Primo took WABC-TV to number one in New York. Then he got promoted away.

18—Thank You, John B. Russwurm

"We wish to plead our own cause. Too long have others spoken for us...."

I was as surprised as anybody when the New York Urban League, in May 1970, announced it was giving the John B. Russwurm Award to eight journalists:

Earl Caldwell, *New York Times* reporter;
Don Hogan Charles, *New York Times* photographer;
Stan Scott, WINS radio reporter;
Ed Bradley, WCBS radio reporter;
Jack Walker, WLIB radio producer;
Daphne Sheppard, Brooklyn editor of the *Amsterdam News*;
Ernest Dunbar, *Look* magazine writer;
and *me.*

John B. Russwurm? Until Livingston Wingate, the League's executive director let me know about the award, I knew nothing about the co-founder of the first Negro newspaper. Or Russwurm's partner, Samuel Cornish, a Presbyterian minister. Or that they named their paper *Freedom's Journal.* Or that they published the first issue on March 16th,

1827. Or that they gave this reason for being: "We wish to plead our own cause. Too long have others spoken for us...." The Russwurm honor revealed yet one more gap in my education. No mention had ever been made of him when I was taught America's history in general, and American journalism in particular.

As for us honorees, I could understand the League singling out the other seven folks for "capturing the vitality and the spirit of John B. Russwurm." The other folks were all well-established in the news business. Some had broken down doors at white mainstream news organizations, or brought distinction to Black owned-and-operated news media. I, on the other hand, had been with *Eyewitness News* for less than two years and my reporter's resume was pretty skimpy. I had no record of "sustained excellence in interpreting, analyzing and reporting of the news." I knew that some of the other folks had practiced their craft at small news operations before moving on to major mainstream news organizations where they made names for themselves. Caldwell, for instance, had paid his dues as a reporter at a couple of newspapers in Pennsylvania and upstate New York before the *New York Times* hired him. Unlike me, none had backed into their work, none had been *accidental* whatever. And as for using "the immense power of the press in advocating equality for all," I was still trying to master the art of "standups" done out in the field, doing my best every day to meet tight deadlines and have a general-assignment story make sense in just two minutes, or less, of airtime.

I wondered how the award judges had chosen to include me. I knew real people were "out there," when I sat at one of the desks in the studio, talking into one of the cameras, but I had never given a lot of thought to who was in the viewing audience. Certainly, I never imagined that watching me on the 6 or 11pm news might be a panel of judges, and that one of them would be Andrew Hatcher, former associate press secretary to President John F. Kennedy. That would have been a very scary thought. Though I knew in my heart of hearts that I didn't deserve the award, I simply showed up and thanked the League for the honor.

African people, forcibly brought to America, enslaved and blended—mostly against their will—with people already here, emerged as a new race: *American Blacks*. And since 1619, Blacks have tried to speak for and about ourselves through sounds and songs, and sermons and verses, and all sorts of ways. Including, rather remarkably, through newspapers: more than two hundred of them published before the Civil War with Frederick Douglass's *North Star* among them in 1847, triple that after the war and into the twentieth century. Robert Sengestacke Abbott, *Chicago Defender*, Ida B. Wells Barnett, *Memphis Free Speech*, Robert L. Vann, *Pittsburgh Courier*, Charlotta Bass, *California Eagle,* and hundreds more as publishers, owners, editors, carrying on Russwurm's mission with papers large and small serving Blacks across the South and into places all across the United States in their Great Migration.

When *Freedom's Journal* failed to be the liberating instrument Russwurm intended, and he got fed up with the treatment of Blacks as second-class citizens in America, Russwurm reversed his previous opposition to Blacks moving back to Africa, and he packed up his family and moved to Liberia.

Any chance I had of deserving the Russwurm Award was purely aspirational. I had to change. I had a lot of work to do—on my thinking, and on my doing.

I saw many an opportunity to act on that aspiration: for instance, when *Right On/CLASS,* a Black–oriented magazine, asked me to cover the first official public appearance of Vanessa Williams, Miss America 1984, the first Black woman to claim the crown in the pageant's sixty-two-year history.

More than a century and a half after *Freedom's Journal* made its debut, I could inform *CLASS* magazine readers that, "Just ten minutes away from where a Black Miss America was signing autographs (in Portland, Maine)," John B. Russwurm had lived in a modest wood-frame house now listed in the National Registry of Historic Places. I could also introduce Gerald Talbot to those readers who didn't already know him as the first Black elected to the Maine legislature in its one-hundred-fifty-two-year history. The "overjoyed" Talbot—as he described himself—told me that Williams's victory was more than just a title, he said, "Because it deals with role models...and attitudes that we can do it whether *it* be contests, jobs or political office."

My article for that magazine was also a chance to report a comment about Williams that came from a middle-aged white housewife. That woman said, "She's pretty and I wanted her to win." The woman added that she was surprised to see four Black women in the pageant. "I didn't know Blacks were allowed in it. I thought they had a contest of their own."

Working Russwurm into an article that I wrote for a Black publication was a tiny, private "Thank you" to the pioneering Black newspaper-owner and his "speaking for ourselves" philosophy. It was a philosophy I hadn't known as Russwurm's, but that I tried awkwardly to articulate in my *New York Herald Tribune* letter bashing its "Ten Negroes" series back in 1963.

Speaking for ourselves, as experience has taught me, carries with it the chance for all involved to learn something they didn't know before.

Eyewitness News reporter

19—Whose Hair Is It Anyway?

You no longer look feminine.

In 1971, I decided to wear my hair natural. I was thirty-three years old, and I was tired of waging war against my hair. Tired of using every trick in the book to make my naturally super-curly—okay—nappy hair, get over itself and go straight. Over all those years, except for a brief span as a bald-headed baby, my hair—at various times—had been hot-combed, pressed, relaxed, oiled, texturized, permed, and Jheri-curled to within an inch of its life. And still, given half a chance, my hair always rebounded, always restored itself to its natural self.

I had grown up in the 1940's and 50's, at a time where everybody from advertisers to employers to romantic partners made it clear that straight hair was the hair of choice. The message to me and millions of Black people with my kind of hair was, "Hey, you folks, get to the back of the beauty line."

So, most of us did what we could to kill the curl. And we stayed as far away as possible from any situation that might expose the truth about our hair. The truth being that it took work to get our hair straightened and to keep it that way for one, two, or three weeks, till the next time we straightened it by whatever means of temporary straightening we used, to play along with the desired picture of ourselves. And we stayed far away from anything like swimming, sweating and rain-showers that might make our hair "go back" to its natural state.

At South High school, I broke the color line of the "S Club," a formerly all-white girls athletic club. But the day after we new members were initiated, I had to skip school. As part of the initiation rites, we had to have axle grease smeared into our hair, and had to swallow a raw egg. I imagined the white girls going home and shampooing the grease away. No such remedy awaited me. My mother took one look at the tangled, greasy mess that was my hair and shook her head. "Honey, I have to go to work in the morning and I cannot be up all night with you and your hair. Just go to bed and tomorrow you'll just have to stay home from school."

In my house, it took half a day for my mother to wash and straighten me and my sister Connie's hair. And that was on a good day. She had only one full day off in her work week and she did not look forward to our twice-a-month hair days. Neither did we. Two tender-headed, cranky kids and a short-tempered, overworked mother with a hot straightening-comb is a bad combination.

For years I didn't swim, didn't go bareheaded in the rain, tried not to sweat above my neck or shower without a cap. And, always, always wrapped my head up at bedtime.

Then the late '50's and early '60's happened. From the depths of the civil rights movement sprung word that "Black is Beautiful." And that included Black people's hair. What had started out with just regular folks in the streets had quietly taken hold. The afro, or natural, was being copied by all sorts of high-profile people from Cicely Tyson to Angela Davis, Andrew Young to Muhammad Ali—activists, actors, athletes, politicians, musicians. It was a movement from the grassroots up, and to my eyes the natural made everybody look good.

When I finally decided to make the change, I didn't broadcast my decision. I just did it. More than changing my hair, I was changing my mind, or, better yet, my mind was changing me.

Gil Scott, one of my best friends and a reporter for the Associated Press and later *The Christian Science Monitor,* had encouraged me whenever I talked about going natural. And it was Gil who turned me on to Bob Keyes. Gil, never one to lavish praise on anybody, said Bob was the best cutter of afro hairstyles in New York City. So, I called Keyes and made an appointment. His earliest opening was on the afternoon of the day before I was to go to Washington to cover Tricia Nixon's White House wedding.

Bob Keyes' small shop was tucked away in a corner of the YMCA on West 135th Street in Harlem. Arriving for my appointment, I tentatively approached the small shop's glass door and saw that the place was crowded even though it was still in the middle of the day. Stepping inside, I was greeted by Curtis Mayfield's sweet falsetto flowing from a tape player near the shampoo bowls. The music added a soulful soundtrack to the non-stop activity of Bob, the thirty-something, slim, light-skinned and soft-spoken shop owner, and four other operators. Wielding scissors, combs, and electric razors, they were expertly washing, cutting, combing, and shaping afros into styles that ranged from close-cropped to big and bushy, with most styles trimmed to a size somewhere in between.

Mothers...their kids...took turns in rows of barber's chairs. Pretty young women in mini-skirts, intense young men wearing colorful African-inspired dashikis and laid-back middle-aged gentlemen in bland business suits came and went before Bob motioned me over to his station.

"I've never worn an afro," I said as I settled into the barber's chair, feeling both apprehensive and excited, as if I were about to lose my virginity.

Slowly, he rubbed his hands over my entire head, parting sections of my straightened hair and rubbing strands of it between his fingers, feeling the coarse roots closer to my scalp. After a few minutes of this, he pronounced my hair fit to be cut.

"Your hair's in good shape," he said in solemn tones. He then proceeded to cut most of it off. I closed my eyes. The moans and groans of a Barry White tune melded with the rhythmic, metallic click of Bob's scissors. "Trust me. I'll give you something you'll like," he said softly, reassuring me. First, he cut off the permed ends of my hair, then he switched from scissors to an electric razor and trimmed the rest, shaping it into a short, neat bush. I followed him over to the shampoo bowl, afraid to look at myself in the mirror nearby.

Warm water rushed over my scalp, next a cool herbal shampoo made my scalp tingle. It felt soooo good. But it did nothing to wash away my doubts. "What if I really hate my hair when Bob gets through?" Over and over again, the thought repeated itself like a broken record playing in my head. I felt a knot tighten in my stomach each time I pictured myself showing up at work with my new look.

Knowing it was too late to announce I had changed my mind, I turned to thoughts of a plan B. Maybe if I really hated my hair, I could call in sick. Or maybe I could rush home to my apartment five blocks away, retrieve one of my old wigs from the stash of fake hair and hot curlers that I kept in a couple of boxes in my bathroom, and wear the wig to my assignment later in the day. Back in the barber's chair, a thick cotton towel tucked around my neck, I watched Bob work on my damp hair. Using a long, metal-toothed comb— an afro pick—he separated the tangled strands of hair, while slowly waving a hair-dryer close to my head and directing a steady stream of cool air through my locks. Now, instead of avoiding the mirror, I couldn't tear my eyes away from the one directly before me. Under Bob's orchestration with the pick and the hair dryer, my afro was taking shape.

Turning his electric razor on again, Bob gave my hair a final buzz. Then he handed me a mirror. Slowly he turned the barber's chair to give me a three-hundred-sixty-degree look. I loved it. It was beautiful. More beautiful than I had imagined it could be. I felt beautiful, too. Proud. And, happy. I couldn't hold back a smile. I had found my "real" look. Or rather, Bob, a thin reserved young brother of very few words, had found it. Like a true artist, Bob had seen what lay hidden within the raw material before him and he had been able to reveal it—sculpt it really—with his scissors and combs. And even though this was something Bob did every day, I could see that he took great pride in his work, in his ability to fulfill his promise to pull off the kind of transformation he had performed on me.

As I paid my bill and gratefully handed Bob a generous tip, I thought about the satisfaction he surely must feel from doing his work so well and knowing that he was one of the best at what he did. I envied Bob. I wanted to be that good at what I did. I wanted to be so good that every time I did a news story, the film and the script would come together in such a way that it would wake people up, wake them up sitting at home in their living rooms watching *Eyewitness News*. I imagined a man jabbing his wife with his elbow as they sat together on the couch watching my news story and him saying, "Honey, did you see that? I never thought of it that way," referring to a story I had just explained. I wanted to break through what a dead-on TV critic once called the electronic wallpaper of TV news. The predictable da-dee-da, dee-dee-dah-dah-dah rhythm of most news stories that become just background noise for someone fixing dinner or doing the laundry. Predictable until something breaks that rhythm. Most times that something is a mistake, a verbal stumble, or a patch of dead air.

Happy and inspired when I left Bob Keyes' shop, I knew I had left more than a pile of permed hair behind. I had also discarded some old notions about being a Black woman. Outside the Y, I headed west along busy 135th Street and over to Eighth Avenue and the subway, stealing a look at myself in every store window I passed. "Yes, yes," I thought. "I did the right thing. I was crazy not to have done it before." I imagined that everyone I passed—men, women, and little kids—looked at me and saw an African princess. Softly, under my breath so nobody could hear me, I sang, "You, you make me feel like a natural woman," doing my best Aretha imitation.

I had been assigned to cover an NAACP dinner at a midtown hotel that day and the news conference preceding it. As I walked into the hotel's grand ballroom where television camera crews, still photographers and local television and newspaper reporters were waiting for the news conference to start, a white, male reporter from Channel 2, someone I liked and respected, looked at me and quickly looked away.

A couple of times I caught some of the other white, male reporters whispering to each other and nodding their heads in my direction. Mostly they just avoided me the way people do when they're embarrassed or don't know what to say. Finally, one reporter broke the ice: "I see you have a new hairdo."

Norm Fein, the 11pm show producer for *Eyewitness News,* wasn't nearly so subtle. When I strode into the newsroom later, heading in his direction, he looked up from the script he had been working on at his desk and blurted out, "What have you done to your hair?"

Norm's own thinning hair, his glasses, and his know-it-all air made him seem older to me than he actually was. He also had a bad eye. I was always curious to know what had happened to his eye, whether it was the result of a childhood accident, or something, but he never volunteered any information and I never asked because to do so seemed too insensitive. Anyway, that eye gave him a look of always squinting, a look he turned on me now.

Norm prided himself on always keeping his emotions under control, never blowing his stack, never yelling at people in the control room or barking at reporters like other producers did when the stresses of the newsroom got to them. Unlike other producers, Norm rarely varied his wardrobe. He wore the same green suit most days. He either didn't care, or didn't know, or didn't care to know that the male reporters, led by one of the co-anchormen, Roger Grimsby, made him the butt of their jokes, and competed with each other to see who could come up with the most stinging put-downs of Norm behind his back. No matter how hard they tried, Norm seemed impervious to their best barbs.

"What have you done to your hair?" he repeated, his voice growing louder as he pushed his glasses further up on his nose and brushed a hand over his bald spot.

On the cab ride from the hotel to the office I had re-lived the reaction of the white male reporters to my hair. Their interest and speculation about my hair had dissipated once the news conference was underway and we all turned our attention to the business at hand.

As I thought about how to handle what I imagined would be a similar reaction at the office, I decided to calmly play down my new look no matter what. But the incredulous look on Norm's face made it hard for me to stay calm.

I remembered the time I had watched Norm examine a picture of Kathleen Cleaver, at the time a leader of the Black Panther Party. The young, radical Robin Hoods out of Oakland, California advocated armed struggle against the "pigs"—their word for the police—and had won admirers in Black neighborhoods in New York and elsewhere when, among other deeds, they provided breakfasts to poor children at the start of their school day.

Norm had picked out Cleaver's picture from a pile of Associated Press wire photos, and remarked, "Not bad," after covering up her huge, billowing afro with one of his hands. Without the hair, the green eyed, fair-skinned Cleaver apparently met Norm's standard of beauty.

"Norm, the way you see my hair now, well, this is the way it *really* is: kinky." I spoke slowly, deliberately. I thought if I stayed calm, I could steer the conversation away from my hair and onto my assignment. "Where are you running my story?" I asked, questioning where my story would be slated in the rundown of the 11 o'clock news show.

But Norm couldn't or wouldn't get past my hair. He couldn't believe he was seeing my real hair.

He didn't understand that he was used to my hair in its chemically straightened state. After several minutes of trying to explain this to him, I finally seemed to wear him down, or so I thought, and I proceeded to brief him on the dinner and news conference. He told me I would have about two minutes for my story, and that it would play pretty high in the show. Meaning, I'd better start writing and prepare to edit my story from the raw film footage as soon as it came back from the lab.

I headed for my cubicle, just a few yards from Norm's desk in the newsroom. But before I reached it, I heard my phone ringing. Al Primo the news director was on the line from his home in Old Greenwich, Connecticut.

"I hear you've changed your hair," he said.

"Yes," I replied, noting with an ominous feeling that the news of my hair had traveled with incredible speed.

"Am I going to like it?" he asked.

Who was he kidding? Primo was calling because he already knew from Norm's call to him that he wasn't going to like my hair.

"I don't know, Al," I said, keeping up my end of the pretense that somehow, he could accept wooly hair on one of his reporters.

"Why don't you watch the show and see if you like it," I continued, speaking into the silence on the other end of the line. He watched it. He hated it. "You no longer look feminine," were the first words out of Primo's mouth when I returned to the newsroom after the show. He had called the newsroom while the show was still on the air, and he was already on the phone and waiting when I got back to my cubicle. I listened to him rattle off his objections to my new look: it didn't suit me; the audience wouldn't like it; it was too militant; it wasn't feminine.

"I liked you better the other way," he said icily.

Primo ended the conversation telling me to change back to the old hairstyle. Before he hung up, he reminded me that I was scheduled to go to the *White House* in the morning— the *White House*. Meaning, he couldn't have me going to the most important address in the nation with my hair natural. Primo obviously wasn't listening when I told him that I liked my hair the way it was now.

I don't remember the bus ride home that night, or getting from the bus stop up to my thirteenth-floor apartment in the Riverbend. I just remember worrying about what I had gotten myself into. I called Gil, my reporter friend, and the only person I thought would understand and try to help me think through my predicament. I talked to him for hours. Whenever I wavered about going natural, Gil had encouraged me to follow my own mind, and now he was saying that he liked my hair and that the station management would look foolish if they forced me to get rid of it. He agreed with me that Primo had a lot of nerve saying I didn't look feminine.

I was crying, upset, and frustrated for much of our late-night conversation. But I decided that night to stick with my natural. I thought I could weather whatever storm my decision would cause. And something else bolstered my confidence: I had just signed a new three-year contract with a no-cut clause favorable to me.

In the days that followed I found that I had a few allies at *Eyewitness News,* though most of the staff appeared to want to avoid taking sides. I heard that anchorman Roger

Grimsby compared my hair to a Brillo pad. It was a rumor I never confirmed, but if it was true, it would have been typical Grimsby. I had no reason to expect Grimsby or any of the other white people at the station to stick up for me and my natural. They didn't have a clue about my reasons for wanting to keep it. They hadn't grown up getting their hair straightened with a hot comb every two weeks. They hadn't stayed out of swimming pools or avoided going bareheaded in the rain because their hair would "go back" if it got wet. They hadn't had their lives limited because of the texture of their hair and the fear that if the truth was known about their hair, they would be looked at as sub-human and made fun of by some people.

Arriving in Washington the next morning, I checked into the hotel and found a stack of messages marked "urgent" waiting for me. They were all from Primo. Any hope I had that, overnight, Primo might soften his resistance to my change of hair evaporated when I reached him in New York. He warned me that if I refused to change my hair, the Tricia Nixon wedding story would be filmed without me in it. What he meant was that I would still do all of the usual newsgathering and write a script with all the relevant information, but viewers would only *hear* me reading my script; they wouldn't *see* me. I would be reduced to being a narrator, only. He added that all of the station's plans to have me do a wedding wrap-up report live in the studio would be canceled. My filmed report would simply run without me in the studio to introduce it, contrary to the "eyewitness" format that called for reporters to be seated on the set and report their stories live after being introduced by the anchors. Primo, the inventor of the reporter-as-eyewitness concept, was saying that he would scrap that concept and its application to the wedding of one of the country's first daughters, rather than allow me to go on the air.

And as further punishment I would also be dropped from the *A.M. New York* morning show, where I was scheduled to make an appearance the following Monday to talk about the wedding with the show's host, John Bartholomew Tucker. Primo kept raising the stakes, but the more he raised them, the more determined I became. I told him I couldn't go back to the old hairstyle because I didn't know any hairdressers in Washington, but that was just an excuse. I had no intention of getting my hair straightened to please him or anybody else. I had told him I *couldn't*, but what I meant was I *wouldn't* change my hair.

On important stories, especially if they are the rare out-of-town ones and costing the station big bucks, a field producer is assigned to coordinate planning with the camera crew in the field and with the local news staff back in New York. Field producers in many cases also work with the reporter on how the story will be written and filmed. Howard Weinberg, my field producer for the wedding coverage, and I had worked together previously on other stories and projects. Howard turned out to be an important ally. After talking things over, we agreed to ignore Primo's instructions to keep me out of the film footage. We shot our wedding pieces in the signature *Eyewitness News* style. Each story opened and closed showing me standing in front of the White House or walking in the Rose Garden. We left it to Primo and the film editors in New York to cut me out of the film and out of my stories.

Meanwhile, at the White House my hair didn't make me a marked woman. As far as I could tell, nobody paid me any special attention; security didn't single me out as a terrorist or political radical or someone to keep under close surveillance. Whenever reporters covering the wedding were briefed, I lined up right along with the *Today Show's* Barbara Walters, Aline Saarinen of NBC, the United Press International's Helen Thomas, and dozens of others—most of them female—to get my instructions on whatever information was being handed out. These briefings included short sessions on protocol and a pre-wedding tour of the Rose Garden where Tricia Nixon and Edward "Fast Eddie" Cox would be married the next day.

There was even a tour of the wedding cake! The cake had been placed on a big round table in one of the White House reception rooms and roped off the way a museum ropes off a work of art. Reporters were allowed to walk around the cake as if it were a masterpiece. And to the people who baked it, I suppose it was.

The cake was described in a press release down to the last bit of icing. But that wasn't enough for some reporters; they managed to come up with questions not answered to their satisfaction in the press release. I couldn't believe supposedly serious reporters could ask so many questions about a cake. Like what *kind* of raisins and how *many* were in it. It was weird, just the kind of thing I thought *Eyewitness News* viewers would get a laugh from, and I included the cake tour and some of the *probing* cake questions in one of my news pieces.

After the ceremony when I spotted a guest outside the White House, having a piece of the cake, I took the opportunity to ask what she thought of it, and she offered me a bite from her fork. That didn't sit so well with one indignant viewer who later wrote a letter chastising me for my shameful and unhealthy act of eating from the same fork as a total stranger. Guess she figured there are limits to being an "eyewitness."

Another highlight of that assignment was trying to get a sound bite from President Richard Nixon. When reporters spotted the President strolling across the South Lawn, dressed in a dark business suit and tie and white shirt, and looking slightly more friendly, I thought, than his sinister, five-o'clock-shadow look on television or the dark, brooding presence in the political cartoons. A pack of us ran after him, trailing our cameras and microphone cords and shouting silly father-of-the-bride questions at him; and recording his predictable answers while the Secret Service kept us at a distance.

"Are you nervous? What's it like to be losing a daughter and gaining a son-in-law? Have you seen the cake? How do you feel?"

I was grateful when the Secret Service shooed us away. Scrambling for a few presidential words seemed as ridiculous as the cake tour. Prevented by protocol from asking any policy questions, we behaved like starving beggars fighting for a few crumbs. We would accept any tidbit to feed the news machine.

I returned to New York certain that I would have to steel myself against what was coming. I had no idea what Primo and the News vice president, Ken McQueen's next move would be. I didn't have to wait long to find out.

Early Monday morning I was summoned to McQueen's second-floor office. The secretary ushered me into what I remember as a surprisingly innocuous-looking office for a vice president and general manager. Not a lot of plaques on the wall, or a tufted leather sofa screaming "this is a male environment," as I would have expected. McQueen and Primo were both standing, smiling. McQueen, whose deep-set eyes and square jaw gave him a rugged cowboy look, motioned me to a chair. Primo took a seat on a couch. After a few pleasantries ("How was Washington? Did you enjoy the wedding?"), they turned the conversation to my hair, and things deteriorated real fast.

"Melba, we simply can't let you go on the air with your hair like that," McQueen said from behind his desk where he sat with his hands folded under his chin. "But I like my hair this way," I replied. "And I've decided that I'm not going to change it."

McQueen soon dropped his friendly pose and glared at me. Primo tightened his flawless white teeth around his pipe. "You're being very stubborn, very foolish," he said sternly as he inspected the tobacco in his pipe. "You don't seem to understand. You're one of our stars. We don't want you to change. We think you're going to alienate the viewers." It was nothing personal, they said. The afro just sent the wrong message. I assumed they meant people might mistake me for a Black Panther. Or maybe my hair, like Tommie Smith and Juan Carlos's raised fist salute at the 1968 Olympics, sent a Black Power message. I could only guess that Primo and McQueen made these kinds of connections with the afro hairstyle and that they feared my hair would scare white people away from Channel 7 news.

Still, I countered each objection with the same argument: "I like my hair this way. I don't see anything wrong with it."

If I wouldn't change my hair, they figured the next best thing would be to cover it up. "You'll have to wear a hat, or maybe a scarf if you want to be on the air," McQueen insisted. "Don't you think that would look dumb?" I asked, stifling a laugh. While McQueen talked, I pictured how I would look showing up on the air in a different hat or scarf every night. I imagined people at home watching me and falling all over themselves laughing because I had turned into the brown-skinned, television news version of Hedda Hopper. She was the Hollywood gossip-columnist who, back in the day, was known as much for her headgear as for her headlines. And given the critical comments that letter-writing viewers—especially women—write to female reporters about their clothes, I might need a different hat for every day.

Once in a while, McQueen or Primo would leave the room, Primo to check up on things in the newsroom downstairs, McQueen, I presumed, to dream up more reasons why the viewers would switch channels if I insisted on keeping my afro. Late in the day, after they ran out of threats and crazy ideas and I had grown tired of repeating my one line about liking my new hair, the three of us just sat in silence, for what seemed an eternity, staring into space.

Nothing I said got through to Primo and McQueen. And nothing they said convinced me to go back to straightening my now-much-shorter hair. Finally, McQueen threatened to keep me off the air entirely, no hat, no scarf, no nothing, just voice only. Or better yet, he said he would assign me to cover landfill stories on Staten Island until I gave in. "You won't be seen again until you go back to your other hairstyle," he warned.

Banning me to Staten Island would have been the same as keeping me off the air because we hardly ever looked to that isolated borough for news. Staten Island was considered the boondocks, too far away from Manhattan to waste a reporter and a camera crew on anything out there short of major mayhem striking the place. Even the other three boroughs, Brooklyn, the Bronx, and Queens seldom got the kind of coverage that local news stations accorded Manhattan.

The meeting in McQueen's office stretched on, with the stalemate lasting for three days, until word of it leaked out to one of the tabloid newspapers. I was back in my office cubicle where I was left to sit all day with no assignments when a reporter from the *New York Post* called me. He said he had heard that I was being kept off the air because of my afro and he wanted to know if it was true. Instinctively, I tried to stall him. I didn't want to make matters worse by talking to the newspapers. And I definitely didn't want my picture splashed across the pages of the *New York Post*. I didn't realize it at the time, but having the *Post* poking around was going to turn the tide in my favor. I told the reporter I had no comment, and if he wanted to check out the story he should talk to Primo or McQueen. A few minutes later Primo rushed into my cubicle. "You're going back on the air, tonight."

The fear of bad publicity ended the stalemate. The *Post* did write a story quoting Primo and McQueen who made light of their feud with me. While the story wasn't the public-relations nightmare it might have been if I had given my side, it did touch off a flood of viewer mail. Some of the letter writers took pains to identify themselves by race and gender. And most of them criticized the station for trying to dictate how I should look. Even people who said they didn't like my hair thought the station had no right to force me to wear a hairstyle that wasn't my choice.

All of this over a change of hairstyle. As I certainly must have known all along, but would come to understand much more, this whole confrontation had not been just about hair. It was about beauty, and femininity, and who had the power to define those qualities. And most of all, it was about image. My image, and who would control it, me, or the news managers at Channel 7?

The hair episode woke me up to the fact that "feminine" to Primo, and to most people making decisions about on-air talent—whether they admitted it or not—meant white women, preferably blue eyed, and blonde with straight hair. That was the feminine ideal reinforced in all the media then, and to some degree still is, to this day.

By choosing my natural hair I was declaring that my taste, my sense of style and propriety had to be acknowledged. Once I understood that I was in a battle over image—and hair was only a part of it—I became determined to be in control of mine. It wasn't my goal to stamp out the notion of one pervasive standard of beauty and femininity that every woman in television should aspire to, but to offer a strong, natural alternative to it.

Al Primo reminisced in his book, *Eyewitness Newsman,* that even he was surprised by the extent of the negative reaction my hair generated in the upper ranks of company executives. By Primo's account, the man he reported to, WABC-TV Vice President and general manager, Ken McQueen, said in an angry phone call, "*Everybody's* upset about this. I have to do something." Primo says it occurred to him then that McQueen was being pressured by his superiors. McQueen in turn tried bringing the hammer down on Primo while making it clear how he felt about me and my hair. Primo writes:

> McQueen's voice rose and cracked as he said, "When I saw her on the news last night it scared the hell out of me. I wanted to jump behind my couch and hide."

What might have frightened McQueen was not my natural hair, but what it represented. I was freeing myself of the responsibility to look good for the executives. Maybe he feared that my freeing myself of the tyranny of "good hair" and chemical straighteners was just the beginning of establishing a new standard of female beauty. Maybe he was scared that I would become his Kathleen Cleaver, good-looking if you just pretended her hair wasn't kinky and too much if she insisted on being herself.

"It's an ill wind that blows no good," my mother often told Connie and me when she wanted us to look for something good when life hands you something you'd rather not have. Her wisdom was proven with the hair squabble. At the time of the blowup, I was the host of *People, Places and Things,* a weekly, half-hour WABC-TV public-affairs program. I thought the program gave me a chance to take viewers on a quick survey of "The African Influence on American Style." That title came easily and reaching out to colleagues and friends, I had no problems producing segments on the roots of the natural hair choices of not just me—by everyone from Andrew Young and Muhammad Ali to Cicely Tyson, Barbara Jordan, and anonymous folks in all walks of life. Viewers met Karen Baxter, a young woman hair-braider who lived and worked out of her home in Harlem. I filmed her plying her trade on my head and talking about the braiding tradition while her fingers flew.

I shot other pieces on African-inspired jewelry with artist and designer Vincent Miller, and on clothing with the owner of Knobkerry, a Manhattan boutique. And my film crew and I went to Bedford Stuyvesant Restoration Corporation in Brooklyn to do a segment with Design Works on hand-crafted African-inspired fabrics being reproduced for home furnishings.

As I tracked down people to interview, and discovered how rich the topic was, I could hardly wait for the finished program to air. I just knew the audience would share my excitement about the subject matter and the new people that most of them would be meeting for the first time. This program promised to be a great learning experience on both sides of the camera, for the audience and for me.

And I thought back to Bob Keyes, and the satisfaction he got from his work when it changed someone in the way they saw themselves in the world. This was one of those times for me.

20—Are You Satisfied Yet?
Do You Mean Sexually?

"The Stones are in town. Take the crew and head over there," barked the assignment-desk editor, shoving a press release at me. He turned and scrawled my name on the big chalkboard at the front of the newsroom where he kept track of reporters and the stories they were covering.

"Who the heck cares about the Rolling Stones?" I grumbled, scanning the press release and noting the address of our destination in Manhattan. From the front seat of the crew car, I asked the question again and checked the rearview mirror expecting a rise from the sound man or the lighting guy in the back seat. The lighting man grunted but kept his nose buried in the morning tabloid. Crew hierarchy determined the seating arrangements; reporters claimed the passenger seat next to the cameraman behind the wheel. Mine wasn't talking. His eyes were on the road. I swallowed the last of the bad coffee from a paper container. "The Rolling Stones! Humph!"

The press conference room was already jammed when the crew and I arrived. We found a spot in the line of cameras set up on tripods and squeezed in between the crews and reporters from our local TV station competitors. All around us radio folks with tape recorders, and reporters and writers from what seemed like every newspaper and music magazine waited. And down front from us crouched around the table where the Stones would sit, still photographers, cameras in hand or hanging from straps around their necks, jockeyed for position. My sound man positioned our microphone with its bold Channel 7 logo in the middle of a nest of mics on the table behind a low flower arrangement, gave it a few quick taps to make sure it was working, then passed me a hand mic. The reporter's notebook and press release in my other hand were proving useless in the dimly lit space where I contended with shifting bodies and sharp elbows.

The wild scene grew even crazier with all kinds of pushing and shoving when the Stones made their way into the room. Of the five skinny, shaggy-haired musicians shielding their eyes from the glare of the TV lights, I recognized only Mick Jagger's face with its generous lips. But I was at a loss as to who was who when Keith Richards, Charlie Watts, Mick Taylor, and Bill Wyman seated themselves behind the mics and began to take questions.

Half a dozen reporters raced to be first. After the initial queries about the Madison Square Garden dates, reporters tossed questions right and left about expectations for the rest of the tour. At one point Mick Jagger announced plans for a free concert in California—location to be determined—later in the tour. More questions about the music, about plans for new recordings...on and on it went. Reporters who knew all about The Stones showed off their expertise. The rest asked follow-up questions, trying to outshout each other. Soon all the obvious ground—the press release stuff—had been covered.

My earlier grumpy mood had lifted. I was now desperate to pose a question. It wouldn't do to go back to the newsroom and have only the questions asked by other reporters on my film track. I needed to have my own voice heard on the track asking at least one question. But what? Anything I thought I knew about the group had been covered already. I sensed time was running out. If I didn't think fast the conference would end, and I would miss my chance. What could I ask?

I waved my mic in the direction of The Stones like a kid in class trying to get the teacher's attention. One of The Stones spotted my mic. "You," he said pointing in my direction. Settling for the one fact I knew, my mind presented it to me and I spit it out: "One of your most famous songs is about satisfaction. Are you satisfied yet?" Mick Jagger, looking amused at first, composed a straight face and shot back, "Financially dissatisfied, sexually satisfied, philosophically trying." A roar of loud laughter rocked the room and Jagger curled his large lips in a huge, satisfied grin.

Back at the station, when my piece played near the end of the evening news program, the cameramen, reporters, and anchors in the studio also cracked up watching Jagger's reaction to the disembodied voice asking a question from the bowels of the dark press conference room.

Who would have guessed that decades later, people—me included—would still be laughing at my desperation question and Jagger's sly reply. Thanks to two documentary filmmakers, Albert and David Maysles, they are.

Who knows if the Maysles brothers tuned into our news show that night by chance, or someone tipped them off about my exchange with Jagger. Whatever the case, the Maysles chose to use that light moment in their landmark rock-and-roll tour film *Gimme Shelter*.

They also captured a much darker scene on film. Their cameras were rolling at the Altamont Speedway in California later that year when thousands of Stones fans turned a free concert into a free-for-all. As some concertgoers surged onstage, someone from the Hells Angels security, hired by The Stones to keep order, stabbed a man to death.

Rock historians and bloggers still write about *Gimme Shelter*. One critic describes what he calls a "double bounce" scene in the finished documentary. He writes of Jagger sitting with the film's editor, and the two of them being filmed as they watch the press conference footage. All of this edited together, and Jagger exclaiming "That's bullshit," as he watches himself trying to be charming and glib with a female reporter who has asked, "Are you satisfied yet?"

I did feel a deep satisfaction, personally and professionally when I had a chance to cover a very different musician. Stevie Wonder in 1973 was to release his new album, *Innervisions*. The press had been invited to show up at a designated spot in midtown Manhattan, and once we got there, we were ushered onto a bus and blindfolded. Not my camera crew, of course, because they were filming everything as the bus driver drove up one street and down another, making a turn here and another turn there. This went on for about twenty minutes—zigzagging around midtown—before the bus stopped and we were ushered off, blind-folded, still not knowing our whereabouts.

Someone then led me and the other reporters up a flight of stairs and into a room. We were helped to lower ourselves onto pillows. We sat on the floor and listened to songs from the new album. We were invited to help ourselves to small bowls of nuts and dried fruits, soft drinks and other treats that had been placed on tables near us. When the album ended, we were told to remove our blindfolds, and there was

Stevie, in person, in dark glasses, waiting for us to do our individual interviews with him.

It was not my first interview with Stevie. He was in New York to do a concert and staying at the Fifth Avenue Hotel the first time I met him. Instead of setting up in his room, my camera crew and I decided to do the interview in Washington Square Park, a Greenwich Village landmark of chess players and amateur musicians, in the middle of the New York University campus. With Stevie and me seated on a park bench and the camera rolling, Stevie worked his signature sense of humor and opened the interview by singing—a cappella—a little song about the *Eyewitness News* team. He had made it up on the spot; it was clever, poked fun at us and was right on the money. His interview was a model of how to be totally present in the present.

Now, with my blindfold story, as with so many others I was cutting things close. I had to wrap up the interview, get back to the office, brief the producer, get settled in at my cubicle, write my script before the film was developed and delivered and set up in editing. Those were the days of sixteen-millimeter film, before videotape! As I sat at my desk, listening to Stevie's voice on my tape recorder and replaying in my mind the street sounds from the bus ride, the feelings of uncertainty and dependence while I was blindfolded, and the music I had first listened to less than an hour ago, I considered some of the ways I might piece together all the different parts of my story. Finally, I settled on how to tell the story best with a beginning, a middle and an end, in two-and-a-half minutes. At least that was better than the two minutes he originally allowed.

"Please, give me just a little more time to let the music play up full," I begged. "I need enough time for viewers to get a taste of the new album," I argued. I wanted to put people in my shoes, I wanted them to experience what I had felt when I was blindfolded. I had discovered what it was like to trust other people to be my eyes. Trust them to help me do things I did every day, like step off a bus, walk along the street, go up a flight of stairs. Help I needed to sit down; the trust I needed to put something in my mouth even when I didn't know what it was.

In the course of things, this wasn't a big story. It wasn't "hard" news, or "breaking" news. It was a story that challenged me to challenge our audience—to get them to imagine being blind. An artist had shared his sightless world with me, an artist whom I admired, personally. He had given me a chance to experience more than just his music. And now I was trying to pass all that on to an audience and do it in just two-and-a-half minutes. I had to pay this feeling forward.

Something else made that initial meeting memorable. Just before I was to go on the 11pm show and air my Stevie story, I got a call from his road manager. Turns out he had once lived in the same apartment complex, the Dunbar, as me and he needed help. The rented vehicle with all of the band's instruments was missing. I made note of all the information and added it to my script. Someone from the rental company got word of my report and got in touch with Stevie's road manager and the vehicle was brought back to the hotel with all the instruments. According to the rental company there was some sort of mix-up and when the vehicle was not returned on time, they towed it back to their lot.

Covering Stevie another time things didn't turn out so well. I convinced the assignment desk to let me do a piece about the release of Stevie's *Secret Life of Plants*. The magnificent glass house in the Botanic Garden in the Bronx was dimly lit, crowded and noisy, great for a press party, but hell for me, trying to move around, gather sound bites and shots of plants in semi-darkness. I tried too hard to tie the songs to some of the plants, of which there were thousands, and my knowledge of even a handful was limited. Almost everything that could go wrong did. The piece aired, but it was a lesson in "how-not-to."

In the end most television news stories come down to: "Go out, find out, tell as much as you can of what you learned and what you know. Do it in a way that gets people to pay attention and do it in less time than it takes to boil an egg."

And even with that I still found satisfaction—sometimes fleeting, sometimes long-lasting.

21—Big Deal

From the New York Times *to the National Women's Conference*

In February 1973, I was the subject of a profile in the Sunday *New York Times*. It recounted my path from secretary to— the article's description of me as—a television superstar reporter. The article, headlined, "Melba? She's the Toast of the Town," described me as "a new kind of celebrity," a television reporter seen by almost a million viewers in the intimate spaces of their homes every night. Some of my comments stepped on a few toes, I was sure though hardly anyone even spoke to me about the article. I said for instance that given a choice, I preferred reporting news to selling brassieres at Macy's. I slammed the copy-cat approach of TV news. As a for instance, the stations, with few exceptions, led with the same stories, aired the same stories at the same point in their programs. I believed they showed little originality of content and little context for what they put on the air. I felt there was little or no connecting of the dots that would allow viewers to understand why certain news was relevant to their everyday lives.

I struck back at executives who kept me off the air when I chose to stop chemically straightening my hair, deciding to wear it natural just days before going to cover Tricia Nixon's White House wedding. Though I later believed I was mistaken and gave credence to a gross generalization when I said what happened with my hair would not have been a problem had there been a Black in authority at the station. Kinky hair is not beautiful to *all* black people. Not then. Not now. Of all the positive letters I received about my hair, only one said my hair was a disgrace. The writer identified himself as a Black man.

In that article I said being Black in a field dominated by white men, was a bigger problem for me than being a woman. Unlike Congresswoman Shirley Chisholm, who ran for president in 1972: her experience was just the opposite. At the time white men ran everything having to do with me and my work. Not white women. I held mixed feelings about the women's movement and stated my opinion that the women's movement had made more progress in six years than Black folks had made since Reconstruction. "I see the women's movement as a white family quarrel." It made all the sense in the world to me that white women who are oppressed are oppressed by white men. White men who wield the power. White men who may be their own husbands, sons, brothers, cousins and so on. Power is the operative word here. And those who use their power against those who have less of it if they are so inclined. To quote the white journalist, David K. Shipler, author of *A Country of Strangers: Blacks and Whites in America*, "Discussions of race are imprisoned by words."

Furthermore, it seemed to me that if white men oppress white women—and others—what role in all of this do the white mothers raising white children play? What values are they instilling in their white sons? What demands are the white women making of their white husbands? Their white uncles and cousins?

Though lost on me at the time, that *New York Times* profile was itself historic, in its own small way. Chester Higgins, the photographer, Barbara Campbell, the article writer, and me, the person being profiled, were three young Black journalism professionals, representative of three different aspects of news coverage. And here we were, on the same page—literally and figuratively—of America's leading newspaper. For an industry whose doors would have been shut tight to us only a few years earlier, this was a sign of media climate change.

The *Times* article caught the attention of Ben Yablonky, director of the National Endowment for the Humanities Fellowship program for journalists at the University of Michigan in Ann Arbor. He thought I sounded like a woman who badly needed to take a break and he and invited me to apply for a fellowship. I replied, "Thanks. But no thanks." Two years passed and I wrote Mr. Yablonky again, asking if I might reconsider his invitation.

When my contract with WABC Channel 7 had run out in the summer of 1976, I'd thought it was time to get an agent and look for a job elsewhere. Just as I'd been making up my mind to leave, yet another news director was being hired. Ron Tindiglia, a short, boyishly enthusiastic red head, was put in charge. Poor Ron. He got caught in a dispute between me and Ken McQueen, the station's V.P.

I'd received an offer from WNBC-TV which my new agent had worked out. It allowed me to accept a fellowship at the University of Michigan and spend an academic year in Ann Arbor (on half salary) before starting work at Channel 4 back in New York, where I would do feature reports and anchor a weekend public affairs program. It was a dream offer.

In Ann Arbor, I joined eleven other journalists, all of them newspaper people, all of us taking a year away from our jobs, and the stresses of deadlines and office politics to study anything—except journalism—that our hearts desired.

Against the advice I got from most people who said, "You're making a big mistake; a year off the air and people will forget all about you," I chose to take that risk and go off to Michigan. I was frustrated with journalism and with myself. I wasn't sure why, I just knew I had expected more.

In the quiet of Ann Arbor, away from noisy newsrooms, impatient assignment editors and the punishing pressures of daily reporting deadlines, the sabbatical had been good for me, even better than I had hoped. The slowed-down days from September through May were filled with field trips and seminars, discussions about art and architecture, classes in American Literature and Black Studies.

I also wanted to look into the racial divide as it revealed itself in American history and literature from the perspectives of a white majority and a Black minority. So, I signed up for two large survey classes representative of the white majority group, and in the Black Studies department, I did history with Harold Cruse, author of *The Crisis of the Negro Intellectual*, and literature with novelist Gayle Jones, author of *Eva's Man* and whose editor was Toni Morrison. Although on the same university campus, the paths of these two tracks rarely crossed; it was as if they occupied two different universes. Kind of like the racial majority/minority divide I witnessed living my own everyday life.

It was a gift of time and space to think and to fill some of the gaps in my formal education. Trained as a nursing professional and learning "on the job" to be a journalist, I worried that I didn't know enough, didn't have the right kind of education to make the most of my situation, to be comfortable in my job.

The sabbatical was a chance to get over feeling inferior to newspaper journalists like those who outnumbered me nine-to-one as fellows in the Ann Arbor program.

Over the months, I discovered that they were a mixed bunch. Just like television-news reporters, their skills varied. Some were smarter than others, and the fact that they worked for newspapers didn't automatically make them more credible or better journalists. And for the most part, they had applied to the program for the same reasons I had: they wanted time away from their newsrooms and hoped they'd be better for the experience.

Another opportunity, that year, totally unforeseen, gave me a chance to collaborate with Dr. Marian Marzolf, a white woman, and the only untenured woman associate professor in Michigan's journalism department. She was looking to create a conference on women and discrimination, and I volunteered to help, not questioning if she was thinking only about white women and suggesting that she might also extend her interest to minorities. She liked the idea and in April 1977, a decade after President Johnson appointed the Kerner Commission to investigate the long hot summer of riots in more than three dozen American cities, Professor Marzolf and I directed Kerner Plus 10: Conference on Minorities and the Media.

That year away was an important turning point for me personally and professionally. That period of study and reflection helped me see how the majority assume the power of definition, especially their definition of others. And the Kerner Conference inspired me to find more ways of including the voices and experiences of everyday people in my reporting.

All of this was excellent preparation for returning to New York and to a new station, WNBC, where one of my first assignments was covering the preliminary delegate state meeting ahead of the 1977 National Women's Conference in Houston.

I can't remember many details of that assignment except that it was in Albany, and I had to hit the ground running. A photo of me taken by Diana Mara Henry caught me seated before a bank of manual typewriters, biting down hard on a pencil, and probably wishing I had just a little more time to work on my story. Positive feedback on the state meeting convinced our newsroom bosses that Houston would be a big deal.

Why did Norman Fein, my news director, and his producers choose to cover a conference happening more than sixteen-hundred miles away and taking a hefty hit to the news budget to do so? I believe it had to do with the temper of the times, the demands of the so-called "women's lib movement," and the ongoing ratings war between local news operations to claim the biggest share of seventeen-million viewers living in our market of New York, New Jersey and Connecticut. What better way to give our station a leg up than having a presence at what was potentially an important gathering of women, and giving precious airtime to, among others, recognizable New Yorkers like Bella Abzug, chair of the event, Gloria Steinem, and Betty Friedan? And why did they tap *me* for the Houston assignment? No one in charge would have admitted that my being female and Black, was a consideration. But they and I knew that I was a "two-fer," slang for one who could be counted and check-offed in two boxes when complying with and reporting to federal regulators and others charged with keeping data on the employment of women and "minorities." Rather, my bosses would have said the assignment was made strictly on the merits, that I was a capable, seasoned journalist

Once the decision was made to cover it, the field producer, Merle Rubine, a white woman, and I got on a plane to Houston and without much planning, got to work. She handled most of the logistics of getting our tapes to the NBC local affiliate for editing and air and checking in with the producers back at 30 Rock. I did the on-camera reporting and interviews, the standups and narration. We sometimes worked together and sometimes went our separate ways, and without walkie talkies or cell phones managed to stay in touch. She went after certain delegates for me to interview and I was scouting out information from various caucus meetings. We called it "crash and burn."

My stories over that weekend aired on both the early and late news. I mixed interviews with narrations explaining the most important and sometimes divisive policies and planks over scenes of caucuses and meetings. I sought to include everyday ordinary women as often as I could in the limited time I had to find them inside the Coliseum. I also talked to women outside and not part of the conference and who opposed the feminist movement in general. The pieces

ranged in length from two-and-a-half to five minutes. My
enduring recollection of Houston is that I was surprised. I
had never witnessed anything like it. I admit I am still
surprised. I thought the personalities that drove the
Conference, and the words and actions that animated it,
were evidence that I was watching—at the very least—the
birth of a new national political party. And I often ask why
things didn't turn out that way.

22—Co-anchors

You cannot put two females on the air as an anchor team.

What were the odds that two girls born in 1938, five-thousand miles away from each other, growing up in very different circumstances, their lives shaped by sometimes similar choices, would be swept along by unforeseen social and political forces and find themselves seated next to each other in a 30 Rockefeller Center studio in New York City as co-anchors delivering the news in the nation's number one TV and media market?

"We want you to co-anchor the five o'clock show with Pia," is how Norm Fein informed me of my new assignment. Norm had preceded me going from WABC to WNBC.

Norm and WNBC had been so eager to sign me after I exited *Eyewitness News* and headed off to a year-long sabbatical at the University of Michigan that they paid half of my salary while I was in Ann Arbor. We agreed that when I returned to New York and to my work for WNBC, I would produce and report three segments a week to air on the 6pm program. *Melba and Company* was to be short profiles of people I found interesting, folks who in different ways characterized our viewership.

We also agreed that I would create and host a half-hour public affairs program to fill a slot on the weekend. I knew exactly what to title the program: *Meet the People*. I thought of it as my attempt to give a platform to regular folks, people who stood out in their circles and in their neighborhoods, but who almost never made it into the media spotlight. To my way of thinking, these were the folks most affected by the decisions and policies made by the bigwigs in city halls, state legislatures, Congress and the White House, the powers that be who always showed up on Sunday morning programs like *Meet the Press*.

Together, *Melba and Company* and *Meet the People*—along with some occasional multi-part special reports—suited me to a T.

None of this however, was spelled out in specifics in my contract.

This was the second time Norm announced that he wanted to pull the plug on my dream job and change my role at WNBC.

The first time, about a year earlier, Fein and his bosses had approached me about becoming one of two females who would take turns sharing the anchor desk with a man, Jack Cafferty. The rotating females would go something like this: Woman One would co-anchor Monday, Tuesday, and Wednesday. Woman Two would co-anchor Thursday and Friday. They would switch the days the next week and keep switching like that.

I told Norm I didn't want to do it. I said I thought alternating the women co-anchors was a crazy idea. "Won't it look like it takes two females to equal one male?" That's how it seemed to me, and I thought viewers would agree.

Fein convinced another female at the station to give the arrangement a try (Carol Jenkins, a smart, seasoned reporter who caused me to even second-guess my own reasoning).

But just as expected, after a few months on the air, the *menage a trois* fell flat.

"The company will remember," Norm warned me, if I refused to go along with his plan.

I reasoned I would be canned anyway even if I went along with Norm's wishes and the co-anchor arrangement didn't work.

Fein and his bosses had some history in anchor arrangements that hadn't worked out. That included a solo male anchor, Tom Snyder, popular and ambitious who left to host a late-night network program. Then two male co-anchors: one of them Carl Stokes, a politician WNBC lured to New York with the promise of a future in TV news. Stokes had made history and news himself when he was elected mayor of Cleveland—the first Black mayor of a major American city—a huge deal in 1968. His co-anchor was Paul Udell, a veteran reporter and anchorperson from California.

Norm's move to pair me and Pia was bolstered by the fact that we were already under contract which meant the company wouldn't have to go out and recruit new people and probably pay them more. We were also experienced field reporters and well-known and respected in the New York area. Plus, before WNBC hired me I had already co-anchored on weekends at *Eyewitness News*.

Fein, knowing his bosses and their superiors would need even more convincing, talked them into investing in a focus group test. He put me and Pia together as one anchor team, and created two other teams with different people and taped each team doing an hour news program. The focus group audience watched and then rated the programs.

"The result for you and Pia was incredibly strong," Fein told me. He said acceptance of us was almost even with Roger Grimsby and Bill Beutel, the white male anchors for *Eyewitness*

News, which was crushing all the competition at six and eleven pm.

In choosing to put Pia and me together, Fein couldn't have picked two people who were more unalike—starting with looks—than brown-skinned, brown-eyed, natural-hair-wearing me and white, blonde, blue-eyed Pia.

"It wasn't that she was white and you were Black," said Fein. "We saw Pia as the worldly sophisticate. And you as the people's person, earthy."

Fein was saying in other words that while Pia and I would share an anchor desk nobody would ever mistake one of us for the other. His assessment of us could have sounded stereotypical to some folks' ears, but I didn't take it that way because I had earned a reputation as a "people person" during my eight years with *Eyewitness News.* It was one of the main reasons WNBC had hired me in the first place—that plus the chance to hopefully weaken *Eyewitness News* by hiring me away from them.

At *Eyewitness News* I had created *Profiles* with one of my favorite producers, Howard Weinberg. He and I would pick a topic—garbage collecting, childcare, the music industry, you name it—and examine it from the perspective of a single individual who might represent the way policies made in Washington, City Hall or corporate boardrooms affects everyday people. I brought the same approach with me when I made the move to WNBC. And when I collaborated on *Consciousness Rising,* an examination of how women from different walks of life viewed the rhetoric of the women's movement that told women it was OK to work outside the home. I brought my own experience to that series drawing on what I knew from growing up around women who ran households and held down jobs, just as my mother who was divorced had done while raising two children.

My mother, Susan Ola Turner of Cave Springs, Georgia happened to be visiting her fiddle-playing uncle Dooley's family in nearby Dalton, Georgia, when she met my father, Emory Leonard Tolliver, a handsome charmer who everybody called E.L. They married not long after that visit. They had me, their first child in 1938, a year that made history books in part because people tuned in to the radio broadcast of *War of the Worlds* panicked when they heard "news reports" from Orson Welles that Martians had landed in New Jersey.

I was named Melba after the girlfriend of one of my mother's brothers. She played piano and my parents might have been hoping I would grow up to be another musical Melba.

My future co-anchor, Pia Lindstrom, was also born in 1938, but three months before me and some five-thousand miles away in Stockholm, Sweden. She too was the first child of her parents, Ingrid Bergman and Petter Lindstrom. Mutual friends had set them up on a blind date thinking Bergman, an eighteen-year-old aspiring actress, and Lindstrom, a dentist seven years her senior, would hit it off. They did. She was impressed by his looks and the fact that he had his own car.

The late 1930's and early 40's were the war years and whether in Cave Springs, Georgia or Stockholm, Sweden the ground beneath people's feet was shifting, whether the people were aware of the changes taking place around the world or not.

In America, writes historian Isabel Wilkerson in *The Warmth of Other Suns*, the biggest, underreported story of the

twentieth century was well underway. It was the Great
Migration, and it would span nearly three decades.

Six million Black people in the former Confederate states
got it into their heads to leave the South and head North and
West. Sharecroppers, former slaves, skilled and unskilled
workers, tradesmen, educated and illiterate, all driven by their
blind faith that a better life waited for them and their children
at the end of a long bus trip or train ride. These migrants shared
dreams denied to them in their present hometowns and villages
under the Black codes, a legalized system of American
apartheid. It was a system that deemed colored people
lawbreakers if they drank from the whites-only water fountain,
sat in the white section of a bus, waiting room or movie theatre,
looked the wrong way at a white person, failed to step off the
sidewalk to let a white person pass, got caught in town after
dark or tried to vote. For such "crimes," a colored person could
be beaten, burned or lynched.

I was two years old when Susan Ola and E.L. acted on their
shared belief that the life they wanted was as far away as they
could get from the South.

In Stockholm, Pia's father was thinking about leaving home, or
at least sending his wife and child overseas to America after
Germany attacked Poland, and France and Britain
retaliated. Lindstrom feared the war might spread and trap his
family in Sweden. Already a successful dentist, he was studying
to earn a doctor's degree, and needed to stay put. But he
managed to get Ingrid, Pia, and the child's young nanny out of
Sweden down through Germany and into Italy where he saw
them off on an ocean liner bound for New York. The family
reunited a year later, but just briefly. Lindstrom moved alone to

Rochester, New York to finish a two-year course that would allow him to practice medicine in the United States.

On the other side of the country Pia, her mother, and Mabel, their Black maid, lived in a small apartment in Beverly Hills. Ingrid Bergman's star was rising with *Casablanca, Bells of St. Mary,* and other films turning her into the first lady of Hollywood.

Like the vast majority of colored emigrants, Sue and E.L. followed family to the North. My grandmother, Cora, and three of her other children, Albert, Rovena and Louise got there first, and after my parents arrived, they all shared a two-family house. My uncle Al went to school and started a dental lab. My father got hired as a chauffeur. Aunt Rovena started a hairdressing business. My mother joined my aunt Louise as "help" in the homes of suburban white families.

Before I was old enough to start school my parents moved again. From Cleveland, they went south thirty-two miles to Akron. My new hometown was headquarters for the Firestone, Goodrich, and Goodyear rubber companies.

My parents set up housekeeping on the North side near my father's sister, Retha who lived in the public housing projects below the viaduct with her three sons.

Akron is where my parents' marriage fell apart.

In 1949, the separation of Pia's parents caused a huge scandal. Bergman had left Hollywood and her husband and daughter to go make a movie with the Italian director, Roberto Rossellini. In the course of shooting *Stromboli,* on the volcanic island of the same name, the actress and the director engaged in an affair which exploded in headlines around the world. Bergman became pregnant which made her illicit romance even more outrageous and turned Bergman from a movie icon to a scorned woman. Everyone from fans to church leaders denounced her. A US Senator from Colorado went so far as to chastise Bergman on the floor of the Senate, labeling her actions "an assault on the institution of marriage."

The attacks were so vitriolic Bergman refused to set foot in America for the next eight years. And a bitter two-year custody battle over Pia made everyone involved targets of a hungry press and a pugnacious paparazzi.

My closest encounter with anything even remotely resembling the paparazzi happened one afternoon in April two years after Pearl Harbor. A roving street photographer snapped a picture of my father in his army uniform, and my sister Connie and me, strolling down Main Street in Akron. The picture cost my father a few cents and my mother carried it in every one of her wallets for the next forty years.

In a letter in 1950, Pia's mother wrote to reassure her daughter that despite all of the ugly press reports and rumors she never said she would give Pia up or never see her again. Still, Ingrid Bergman remained in Italy, gave birth to a son out-of-wedlock, and continued having her movies and private life make headlines.

Considering the difference in my background and Pia's and the people who raised us, what were the chances that I would ever even meet Pia, let alone anchor a news program with her? That I would begin my journalism career on the East Coast of the United States in the late 1960's around the same time she began hers on the West Coast? That she and I would be in the right place at the right time when the civil rights movement, the women's movement, and changes in the law and shifts in people's attitudes would all be at work transforming the cultural, political and social landscape? That the communications media would open some doors just wide enough for a trickle of white women and Black men and women to slip through? That one day we would be working in the same city—New York—at competing TV stations? Or at the same station when the men running it had a problem they thought she and I could help them solve?

What were the odds that my path and Pia's, starting so far apart, would intersect in the way that they did?

23—Meet the Hatchet Man
"You don't have the ego for anchoring"

Two-and-a-half years after he and WNBC hired me away from my old station, Norm Fein was fired, not long after pairing me and Pia Lindstrom, and the company replaced Norm with Ron Kershaw, a reclusive, gap-toothed television news and sports veteran. Soon as I met Kershaw, my instinct kicked in. Too late. I knew I should have put up more resistance to taking the anchor spot. And I recognized Kershaw as the man with the executioner's axe.

"Hey, I was just talking about you," I said when Kershaw strolled into the green room one Thursday following the five o'clock show. I was trying to make light of the fact that a couple of show producers and I had been gossiping. We were the ones caught tattling, but it was Kershaw who looked uncomfortable. Mumbling a greeting in our direction, he poured himself some coffee, lit a cigarette, stayed in the room a few minutes, then left. Kershaw usually looked uncomfortable around staff like us who were holdovers from the previous news director's regime. He only lightened up around some of his cronies—several camera crew members and the new anchor, Sue Simmons—people who he had worked with in Baltimore and who were his new hires at WNBC.

Back in my office I was on the phone and trying to get singer Dionne Warwick for a live studio interview when there was a soft knock on the door. It was Kershaw. As he waited for me to finish the phone call, he fiddled around with a little bag of potpourri I had hanging from a coat hook on my office door. He looked more uncomfortable than he had earlier in the green room. The phone call had been the last thing I wanted to wrap up before going home. I hung up the phone. Kershaw took a seat opposite me on the other side of my desk. I hadn't invited him to sit down. I was tempted to check my watch to signal that I was in a hurry. Instead, I just looked at Kershaw. "I am going to reassign you," he said, getting straight to the point.

My mind went blank. Kershaw went on, "I'm taking you off as anchor of the five and reassigning you."

A long pause, then, "Reassigning me to what? I asked.

"I haven't decided. But I want to reassign you to something you're interested in. Otherwise, it won't work," he said. Kershaw's pale face, and his brown watery eyes looked dead behind large metal-rimmed glasses.

He said he was thinking of assigning me to *The Today Show*. "*The Today Show*," I repeated slowly. I was puzzled. How could *he* put me on *The Today Show?* It wasn't his territory. He was in charge of local news. *Today* was network property.

"Do you mean the cut-ins?" I asked, my voice registering the incredulity of his suggestion. How can he be serious, I thought. The cut-ins are those hurried headlines and news nuggets wedged into the network's morning talk show, anchored by some poor slob at the local station who's been up since three am. Whoever does cut-ins is also expected to turn a story or two for the local evening news before she can go home, grab a bite to eat, hop in bed, racing the alarm clock and get rested before starting the cycle all over again.

Yeah. That was what he meant. He also mumbled something about "special interviews."

He said he didn't like me as an anchor. He didn't say what he didn't like, and I didn't ask.

"Who's going to replace me?"

"Jack Cafferty will do the five with Pia. And Sue Simmons will replace Cafferty at six with Scarborough. I want to have the same anchor team working at six and eleven."

"Have you told anyone else about your decision?"

"Only Cafferty," he said, adding that Cafferty was on vacation for a few days.

"When do you plan to tell the rest of the people?"

He said he wanted to start the new anchor lineup in a couple of weeks.

"I think we ought to decide what I'm going to be reassigned to so that it can all be announced at the same time." In the back of my mind, I was thinking I needed time to sort this out. He had dropped a bomb, and I had to figure out if I could strike back, and how.

My mind was racing. Kershaw continued talking. He said the reassignment could be a good opportunity for me, after all, "Look what happened to Barbara Walters." He was referring to Walters getting bounced as co-anchor of ABC's network evening news show in the mid-70's. Walters had been paired with Harry Reasoner, becoming the first female to share an anchor desk on a network evening news program. The heavily hyped experiment failed. Kershaw was implying that Walters had gracefully accepted the demotion and was still doing her thing at ABC News years later.

I wanted to say, "Look, buddy, I'm not Barbara Walters and you're not Roone Arledge." Arledge was the fabled executive who had transformed ABC's sports division and then its news department with his innovative programming moves. But I kept still. There were long pauses. Several times Kershaw asked, "Is what I'm saying hurting you?"

What a strange question, I thought. It was obvious my reaction was not what he had expected. I didn't say what I was feeling or thinking. I did tell him that I had known instinctively that neither he nor his boss, Roy Meyer, liked me as an anchorperson and that I didn't know why.

Finally, he suggested that we get together after work the next night and have a drink and talk about what I would be reassigned to. "Do you want me to leave the station," I asked, trying to feel him out, to see if there was more to the reassignment than he might want to admit. "No, I don't want you to leave," he said in a flat, expressionless voice. If he had reasons for wanting me to stay, he kept them to himself.

I told him that since we were having this frank talk, now was the time to tell me if he wanted me to go. I also told him that leaving the station would be one of the alternatives I would be considering.

He got ready to go and asked again, "Am I hurting you?"

"No, you're not," I answered firmly.

He said the fact I was not hurt by his decision to reassign me was the reason I wasn't a good anchor. "You don't have the ego for anchoring. You weren't really into the job the way good anchor people are. They would have reacted differently to being told they were being reassigned."

"I'm not about to go out and cut my wrists or jump off the Brooklyn Bridge because you're taking me off the five," I said, my eyes fastened on his face. As he turned to leave, he said, "OK, let's get together tomorrow after the show and go tip a few." I was still standing at my desk, stunned, as he walked out of my office, leaving the door open behind him.

As I left the office that evening, in a daze, I was sure about one thing: I would give Kershaw a fight. I was not going to make it easy for him to take me off as five o'clock co-anchor. No way. I just needed to talk to somebody. Find out my rights.

On the bus ride uptown to Harlem and home I replayed our conversation in my mind.

I thought about Kershaw's suggestion that we "go tip a few." How crazy was that? I thought. The last thing in the world I wanted was to sit in a bar with my enemy, having drinks like we were old friends or even people on the same wavelength. Kershaw was no friend of mine, despite his claim that he wanted to come up with something that worked for me, like giving me the cut-ins to *The Today Show*.

Walking from the bus stop to my apartment building and checking the mailbox, taking the elevator to the thirteenth floor, I let myself into my apartment and sank into the living-room couch, still trying to sort out the exchange with Kershaw. If I wasn't good enough to anchor the five o'clock, why would I be good enough to do *The Today Show* cut-ins? *The Today Show* cut-ins, like the five o'clock news show, commanded a big audience. It didn't add up. Was Kershaw just trying to make my life hell? Having to be at work at an ungodly hour, writing news briefs and doing the quick reads that fit the tiny window of the cut-ins would really stress me out. Kershaw wasn't making it easy for me. Was I supposed to just lay down and die? Accept his judgment of me? Kershaw had no idea who he was dealing with. He thought I lacked the ego to be an anchor. Well, I thought he lacked the vision to see that all anchors didn't have to be alike. I didn't want to be like the "good anchors," as Kershaw defined them. I wanted to be me. I wanted to make my own anchor statement. I wanted to be a different kind. Not the stereotype that Kershaw was used to. I thought anchors could be more than what I saw. I thought I could re-define the role. I wanted to show him and his boss.

It was time to call Ron Yatter, my agent. After talking to him—and learning that Kershaw had told him about moving me before I got the news—I called a couple of close friends. We talked a long time before I finally went to bed where I lay awake thinking. Overnight I pretty much made up my mind to fight the demotion, especially since Yatter had assured me that my contract did not allow for me to be demoted. It said I was to be an anchor. I decided to take my case to arbitration. It was Yatter who also got me a lawyer. The news of my demotion spread quickly around the newsroom and ran in the local newspaper the next day, which was also my last day, a Friday. I went on the air with Pia for the final time. The show opened as usual with the theme music then our introductions, Pia first, then when it was my turn, I said: "And I'm *still* Melba Tolliver!!!!" My small act of defiance was a signal to tell the audience and my bosses that I intended to stand up to Kershaw. The show continued. After we went off the air Pia gave me a small gift. I was quite frosty when she handed it to me. She wasn't to blame for me getting demoted, but I didn't feel friendly to her, or to anyone at that point. I was mad at the whole world. I had been double-crossed. I had reluctantly accepted the anchor job in the first place only after a lot of arm twisting by the previous news director and general manager. And this was my reward. Here was the upstart white guy who knew nothing about me, telling me he was going to move me.

After the show Sue Simmons came to my office wearing dark glasses. She said she was sorry I was being taken off the five. I was just as frosty with her as with Pia. I didn't offer her a chair. I thanked her and just waited for her to leave. I had tried to be friendly with her when she first arrived at Channel 4, inviting her to dinner at the steakhouse right next door and upstairs at 30 Rock. While we were waiting for our food, she said, "Some friends of mine say you don't like me." What friends? I should have asked. And what's their evidence for saying that? I think I was naïve to expect Sue to level with me. She was, after all, a Kershaw ally. And in the months she had been with the station, she had never shown any signs of wanting to be friends.

When I left the office on my final day as co-anchor of the five, I stayed away for about two weeks. This was another way of showing that I wasn't going to play by the company's rules. I left it to Yatter to inform Kershaw that I was taking my case to arbitration and that I wouldn't be coming in for a while.

During my self-imposed absence, first Bob Teague and then Carl Stokes called me at home and, they advised me not to take the demotion personally. Both men said I should understand that what happened to me was just par for the course in television news. They had both gone through something similar. Stokes, who had been imported from Cleveland after serving as mayor there, had experienced his own demotion from a co-anchor spot at Channel 4. He had been brought in especially to co-anchor, and when that pairing didn't move the ratings dial, management pulled the plug and started a different group of anchors.

Bob Teague was a different story. He had more credentials as a news man than anybody on the staff. Teague had worked for the *New York Times*, when you'd have had to search high and low to find a Black person working in the newsroom of any prestigious paper like the *Times*.

I listened to Bob, and to Carl. But I chose to stick to my decision to stay away from work until I felt I had showed Kershaw and company that I was no pushover. I wanted them to know that they couldn't just move me around anywhere and anytime they pleased.

Within days of making that choice, I turned for help to someone I thought I could trust, a lawyer who was the brother of my best friend. He went with me to meet the lawyer that my agent, Ron Yatter had lined up. The meeting didn't solve anything. I was more confused than ever about what route to take. I had decided to go to arbitration, but maybe I should sue WNBC. A former WABC colleague had chosen that route in his fight with another local station and been successful. My friend's brother wasn't much help. Worse, he hit on me when he brought me home from the meeting. We kissed in my kitchen. The kiss was nice, but it wasn't helping me decide what to do. After nearly two weeks away from work, I got a registered letter from Kershaw threatening to fire me for insubordination if I didn't return to work.

I returned. My first day back in the newsroom wasn't the nightmare I had imagined while I was at home plotting my future and thinking of the nasty treatment that lay in store for me. I came to the office and reported to Bob Davis, the assignment editor. We knew each other from Channel 7 and had no beef with each other. Bob sent me out with a crew to cover the transit strike then in progress. Mayor Ed Koch and some officials from the bus and subway system were walking across the Brooklyn Bridge making their way into Manhattan when I caught up with them. As I neared the Mayor, he stopped long enough to ask, "How're you doing?" He had apparently read about my fight with the station. I assured him I was fine. That question coming from Koch, was amusing because it had become his trademark to ask anyone within earshot, "How'm I doing?" a big Cheshire-Cat grin lighting up his face. Koch could usually count on a positive reply, especially in his first administration when he was quite popular with the press and with most New Yorkers.

After I got through my first day back on the job, the ice was broken, and things pretty much settled into a routine. I got assignments, went out with camera crews, wrote, recorded, and edited my stories and went home. One memorable assignment that stretched into a few days was the Metropolitan Opera murder. A female violinist had been found dead in the bowels of the opera house. I covered that story for quite a while, until investigators zeroed in on her killer, a young stagehand.

Around that time, I also began wearing my hair in twists. Ruth Sanchez, who had a shop on Columbus Avenue on the West Side of Manhattan was my hairdresser and I struck up a friendship with her. She was Puerto Rican and when we met, she was being initiated into the religious practice of Santeria which required her to dress in white from head to toe. Even in New York, a beautiful woman outfitted like a virgin was strange. It piqued my curiosity, and I questioned Ruth. In all my years in New York I had never heard of Santeria; I thought most non-Hispanics hadn't either. That prompted me to do a story about this African-based religion which had originated in Cuba and Brazil and gave devotion to Yoruba gods and Catholic saints. In the process of doing the story, my interviews took me into new parts of Manhattan and the Bronx, boroughs I thought I knew so well. It was eye-opening to learn how widely Santeria was practiced in New York's huge Hispanic community. That story led me to do a whole series on religious practices in the city.

Losing my anchor spot and getting back to street reporting let me see what I had been missing and what I liked most about being a reporter. I had missed coming up with my own stories, stories that often showed up by chance in my everyday life. Like my coming across Ruth and discovering an aspect of Hispanic culture, the sort of thing that hardly ever made it into local news coverage. I usually found it pretty easy to do these kinds of stories because assignment editors and show producers are always on the lookout for story material that wasn't run-of-the-mill stuff that every other station was also bound to be covering. None of our competitors had run a series or even a stand-alone story on religion at that time, and certainly not anything on Santeria.

When my case went to arbitration it lasted for two days. I lost. I should have anticipated the outcome. As someone said later, talent contracts were standard boilerplate once you read past the first couple of pages. And under our contracts, all the rights belonged to the company. I was so naïve. And I failed to do due diligence. Kershaw attended the arbitration hearings, treating them like a minor inconvenience and not a serious threat to anything he cared about. He sat in the back of the room and read the newspaper during much of the proceedings. I testified and so did Kershaw. The judge seemed impassive.

When the whole thing was finished, I ended up with the bill. A big bill. I had to pay the arbitrator and my lawyer. That was the final straw. I decided that I'd had it with everyone. I figured that since the William Morris Agency had given me bad advice, they should foot half the bill. Furthermore, I told them I was putting a stop to their commissions from my salary until they agreed. That's when the William Morris folks threatened to sue me. I didn't care anymore. Let them sue me.

My mother had become ill with breast cancer, a reason, according to Yatter, that William Morris didn't go after me more vigorously for cutting off their commission payments.

My fight with William Morris went on for months. After going back and forth they did foot half of the lawyer's fee, but that wasn't enough in my view. I was still stuck with the arbitration bill. It was on their advice that I went for the arbitration. Plus, I had been misled about my contract. Whether the agency knew better, or was just trying to humor me, I thought they had failed in their job of giving me good representation. As far as I was concerned, they had just been collecting money for not much work. After all, WNBC had been anxious to hire me away from WABC *Eyewitness News* and I could have gotten a job there without Yatter's intervention. I had no quarrel that the agency deserved to be compensated for getting the terms I wanted. Once the deal was made, they did nothing for me, really, after that except collect ten percent of my salary.

So, I decided I would be better off without William Morris. I decided to go to the head agency guy in New York and make a deal. Before meeting at his office, I came up with what I thought was a figure fair to both of us. With that number in mind, I told him I was not satisfied with the agency representing me and thought it was in the best interest of both of us to go our separate ways. He agreed, and also accepted my number. I had the check already made out and handed it over to him. And that was the end of me and William Morris.

Yatter never spoke to me again. I'm sure he was angry because I went straight to the top guy to settle things. I decided I was through messing around with people who were only looking out for themselves, for their own interests. I saw that I was going to have to stand up for myself. I would have to make my own decisions and live with the consequences.

Choosing to go to arbitration and losing further soured my relationship with Kershaw and his bosses at WNBC. But they were not about to fire me. That would have been an awful PR move, even though I'm sure that Kershaw and his boss, Roy Myers, had considered giving me the boot. So, with a year-and-a-half left on my contract I became a general-assignment reporter with an anchorwoman's salary. My only reward for having rebelled against the bigwigs: they still had to pay me. We had both made our choices and we moved on from there.

Once I chose arbitration over keeping quiet and leaving my future in Kershaw's hands, I knew my contract would not be renewed. It was only a matter of time before I would be let go. So, when Kershaw said he wanted to see me as the date neared for my contract to end, I wasn't surprised. It took about five minutes for him to deliver the news, and about as much time for me to tell him about a recent dream I'd had. In that dream, I told him that I forgave him for demoting me. I said I realized he would not want me around once I made the choice to go to arbitration. But as in my dream, I was not holding a grudge against him. I gave him a hug and that was that.

Leaving his office, I passed the desk of Terry, his secretary. A fixture at Newscenter 4, Terry had seen a long parade of news directors and reporters come and go. So, I was quite moved when she stopped me and said she was very sorry I was being let go. I told her it was OK and thanked her for her kind words.

I received a three-month's severance from WNBC and then I was out the door. I felt I had little to be angry about after the Channel 4 episode. In fact, I was grateful to be away from there. In a way, Kershaw had done me a favor.

Now what?

Neither he nor I could have foreseen that three men who had previously been my news directors would bring me into a new venture of which they were a part. Cablevision owner Charles "Chuck" Dolan saw the possibility of a twenty-four-hour cable news service devoted to Long Island and its unique identity separate from New York City. Modeled after Ted Turner's CNN but on a local level, he even had an alumnus of CNN already on staff as an anchorman, Bill Zimmerman. I was brought in with Bill to be founding co-anchors of News 12 Long Island.

Interviewing Governor Mario Cuomo, News 12 Long Island

24—Where Are You Now?

Between WABC, WNBC, and News 12 Long Island, there were periods when I was off the air for many months, in one case (the time between WNBC and News 12) almost five years. Yet people still stopped me on the street, in subways and supermarkets to ask me the same question: "Where are you now?"

At first, I tried simply telling them I no longer worked in television. Almost every time, they would give me a funny look and wait, expecting me to explain. "I'm just not doing that anymore," I'd say. "Oh, that's too bad, you were so good," said some questioners who spoke in soft comforting tones as if consoling someone whose best friend had died.

After a while, I tried joking with my questioners. "Where am I? Right here," I would say, knowing that response could sound sarcastic if I wasn't careful. That still didn't stop the questions. "But I mean where are you? Who are you with now?" they would ask, as if I didn't get the question the first time. "I'm not with anybody. I don't work in television news anymore," I'd reply. At those times I often felt like a failure. I was no longer working on the air at the station where they last saw me. And I didn't have a job at another station where they could tune in to see me. It wasn't good enough for me to be standing in front of the person, live. They felt sorry for me. And I felt like a disappointment to them.

Finally, I just gave up on explanations, jokes, and answers people found not satisfying. But inside I was angry. Angry because I got tired of explaining myself. Angry because I realized I had paid a big price for going into peoples' homes night after night for years. Some people began to think they knew me. They thought I belonged to them. I had become like a member of their family. And when I disappeared from their television screens, regardless of the fact that my departures were usually noted in the newspapers and that here I stood right in front of them—a living, breathing person—my questioners acted like they had lost someone close to them.

I didn't understand that. No one had warned me of the crazy one-sided relationship that viewers would form with me, someone they knew only from what they saw on screen. Having been on television as regularly and for as long as I had been, it seemed that my image was burned into the tube. And until that after-image burned out, dimmed by time, I was stuck.

It's what I came to think of as the Anwar Sadat syndrome.

The day Sadat was killed I was listening to the news on the radio, and like millions of people around the world, I was shocked, touched, and horrified with each news bulletin. I hoped that maybe he had only been wounded by the shooter, that he would be OK.

But soon it was clear that the man whose face had become so familiar to me that I felt I knew him, had paid with his life for trying to make peace with his enemy. When I turned from the radio to television the pictures of the assassination scene put the final stamp on things. Yes, Sadat was indeed dead.

News correspondents appeared on the air live and cutting to videotaped pictures of the bloody assassination scene. The news bulletins soon began to carry clips of a live

Sadat at Camp David with President Carter and Israeli Prime Minister Menachem Begin. The clips included closeups of Sadat, dark and smiling and talking about peace in the Middle East. Through modern technology the man could be dead one minute, shot down in the bloodbath that took place in a military reviewing stand, and alive the next minute in the mountains in America, looking me in the face through my television screen, talking to me about peace. Alive in one picture, dead in the next.

Television had made it impossible for Anwar Sadat to be dead that day. How could he be dead when there he was, right up there on the screen? Through the miracle of television and tape, a man who had just been riddled with bullets couldn't be allowed to die.

Television created an instant afterlife. On television a dead Sadat kept coming back to life.

In my case, no tapes are re-run showing me as I used to be, covering fires and funerals and Christmas tree lightings and all of the stuff of local news. But the image was still burned into the tube for a while. I think that is what makes people ask, "Where are you now?" when I'm standing right in front of them. So, when I say, "Here I am," it doesn't register, because to the person asking the question it is as if I'm not real unless they're seeing me on their television screen.

* * *

And so, here we are, where I first started writing this book, hoping it pays tribute to the amazing grace and wisdom of ordinary, everyday people like the ones who raised me.

I also hoped this book would be a way of sharing and illuminating my belief that each of us is unique. And each of our lives is full of wonder. All that's asked of us is that we stay awake and aware of the constant interplay of chance, choice, change, and connection.

Appendix—An Angry Woman

Letter to National Correspondent Robert S. Bird.
Published May 1963 as part of the New York Herald
Tribune *series, "Ten Negroes"*

Dear Mr. Bird,

What happened? Did you find the lake of Negro opinion too chilly for the nice long swim you intended? You certainly dived in with all your might with the lead-off article on the Black Muslims. Then, as your series on the "Ten Negroes" progressed, it seemed as if you decided to get out of that cold river of controversy as rapidly as you had dived in.

What happened? Weren't you able to find any interviewees who could or would give you the real reasons for the bitterness. disenchantment, and despair of the Negro in America? Were you unable, in all your travel and investigation, to find just one Negro who could or would tell you what it's like to be an American Negro?

I cannot believe that you could not find one Negro who could tell you what it's like to walk down the street in a predominately white community with all of the stares and whispering. I cannot believe that you could not find one Negro who could tell you of all the little things that happen to him every day of his life on his way to work or school. All of the small things that are a prelude to his work or school day. The things that he accepts, but not quite. The multitude of his "small" things that sink into his unconscious self, but display themselves in his early morning scowl and his pre-coffee grumpiness. The "minor" things that cause his white co-workers to wonder why Miss or Mr. Negro is so "darned evil."

Mr. Bird, I would rather believe in the things stated in the United States Constitution, the Bill of Rights and the Supreme Court Decision of 1954 than believe that you could not find just one American Negro who could shed some real light on what it's like to be a Negro in the United States.

For the past week I, and others like me, have been waiting patiently to see one white person, through a series of profiles on ten Negroes, enlighten other members of his race on the reasons why the Negro feels and acts the way he does. I, and others like me, have been sorely disappointed. Negroes have not been disappointed in the same way as whites have been. We have not been expecting you to tell us things that we did not know, for we are intimately knowledgeable about the things you wrote and did not write, as well as the most minute goings-on in the lives of most white people. Not, in the case of the latter, because we want to but because we have had no other choice.

Yet, in all this time no one has wanted or tried to know anything about us. No one cares when they run those beautiful shampoo commercials that we have kinky hair, most of it black with no hopes of finding out "whether blondes have more fun." No one cares if our hands never become "soft and white" no matter how many jars and bottles of "Brand X" we use.

I won't waste the time, Mr. Bird, to go on with this little story because the things I have just written about are only 1/100,000,000,000 of the many things that go into the making of a bitter, disenchanted, and despairing Negro.

The invisible man that no one knows or cares about. The invisible man that the white world wishes would completely disappear and solve the "American Dilemma."

But we're not going anywhere, you know. We're here to stay. That's why I, and so many others, are disappointed, Mr. Bird. Because you had the opportunity to shed some light on America's "dark problem" and you failed, you failed miserably.

As we say "uptown," Mr. Bird, why didn't you "come on down front and tell it like it really is?"

Cordially,
MELBA TOLLIVER

P.S. Miss Calloway wasn't too much help either when she said, "she forgot she was a Negro." The majority of us are not seeking to forget, but rather a little remembrance on the part of white Americans!

Acknowledgements

Many people supported me over the years of writing this book. I am deeply grateful to all of them. I extend a special thank you, for nurturing my mind, body, and spirit, to:

Lisa Jackson   Ethel Drayton-Craig, Ph.D. Regina Marinelli
Bart and Phyllis Palamaro   Sheila Page   Al Ittleson
Hugh Hammett, Ph.D.   Natalie Goldberg
Marion Marzolf, Ph.D.   Professor Gary Goss
Mildred Fleming   Lynnie Godfrey   Nancy Larsen
Cherryl Thomas, M.D.   Robyn Hooks   Arnold Stovell
Greater Lehigh Valley Writers Group   Peter Coyne
Leah Komaiko   Rick Williams   Jerry Waxler
Israel Zighelboim M.D.   Dr. Nicholas Cardiges M.D.
SUNY Empire State College   Deborah Durham
Virginia, Clemente, and Tyriek Ettrick
Hwesu Samuel Murray

Special thanks to enlightened journalist Robert S. Bird, 1904-1970, who was able to see his own blind spot, and to

Gwen Ifill
1955-2016

I never met Gwen Ifill. I read her journalism in newspapers and admired her from afar before she brought her keen insights and steady grace to television news. Along the way, and to my surprise, she paid me the highest compliment. That she found me to be a role model was humbling, yet reaffirming of my belief that we are indeed all connected. Endometrial cancer took Gwen's life and has threatened, but spared mine, so far. This, too, is humbling.

MELBA TOLLIVER reported and anchored news at
WABC-TV, WNBC-TV, News 12 Long Island and the Food
Channel, in addition to writing for *USA Today, Good
Housekeeping, Black Sports,* and other magazines and
newspapers. She was host and reporter for the ABC Network
series, *Americans All;* and for several WABC *Eyewitness
News* series, among them, *Profiles, People, Places and
Things,* and *Consciousness Rising.* She was writer/producer
of "Gordon Parks: Man for All Seasons," for the WABC
public affairs program *Like It Is.* At WNBC, Tolliver created
and hosted the public affairs program *Meet the People.*
Tolliver served as Howard R. Marsh visiting professor of
journalism at the University of Michigan and was writer-in-
residence at Pratt Institute. She has been recognized with an
honorary Doctorate of Humane Letters from Molloy College,
a Lifetime Achievement Award from the New York
Association of Black Journalists, the John B. Russwurm
Award from the New York City Urban League, the Matrix
Award from New York Women in Communications, and a
National Endowment for the Humanities Fellowship to the
University of Michigan, where she co-directed Kerner Plus
10, a conference on minorities and the media.